Games and Activities
for
English Lessons

Illustrations by
Cornelia Kriechbaumer

ISBN: 9798733502397

Table of contents

Preface

'Sorry! We can't play games today – we have to learn something!'

This is an imaginary quotation, but it is worrying to imagine how often it might be heard in classrooms. Games, while being fun, are usually linked to the ideas of relaxation, something you do after work (i.e. once the real work is finished) and not necessarily to be taken seriously. There is no doubt that language learning is hard work. But this does not mean that games are independent of learning.

This book is a collection of games, creative activities and puzzles that I have found useful in the course of my teaching career. It is certainly by no means anything approaching comprehensive, nor is it meant to be. There are any number of publications to be found offering ideas for games. Many of the activities in this book are followed by a number of variations. The focus is intended to lie just as much on the economic use of ideas and materials and on the ways in which they may be adapted, as on the ideas themselves. In passing on these ideas, I hope that the user may have as much fun in their classes as I have had over the last 34 years.

Introduction: What, who, why and how?

What?

So, what do we mean by a 'game'?
There are many books on the subject of games in the language classroom, not all of them define in any detail what exactly a game is, or what the characteristics of a game are, but take it for granted that we all know what a game is. Ur (2016, p. 26) states that games 'should involve some kind of fun challenge'. This can be against opponents, in the form of a single opponent or an opposing team, but can also be a 'task that is obviously easy, but whose achievement is limited by rules'.

Wright et al. (2006, p. 1) define the essential element of a game as that of being 'meaningful, engaging and ... challenging. Competition against others is not an essential ingredient of games, but challenge often is. '

Ur (2014, p. 2) adds that a discussion can be made more productive by adding the element of a 'task', which is defined as 'a process aiming to achieve a clearly expressed outcome', but adds that that there are activities which can be motivating without necessarily having a task to achieve.
In addition, the distinction between 'game' and 'activity' is not always clearly defined. Harmer (2001, p. 135), for instance, when describing forms of communication in the classroom, mentions communication 'games' and 'activities', without defining either.
The dividing line between 'game' and 'not-game' is not a clearly defined one. Meighan (2011) uses games as a sub-category of activities, whereas Buttner (2007) has games and activities as separate categories. Indeed, it seems that sometimes the label 'game' is attached to many activities in the hope that the label itself will provide motivation for an otherwise monotonous and uninteresting task. One

humorously intended explanation comes to mind here: 'If it's fun then it's a 'game', interesting then it's an 'activity', and if it's neither of these it's an 'exercise'.'

A word on correction: Correcting students' errors has to be done with tact and sensitivity at the best of times, and especially in a situation where the students are focussing on having fun, continually interrupting a game to correct mistakes of form is going to turn them off playing any games very quickly. However, we have to remember that the teacher's aim is for learning to take place as well as providing an opportunity to have fun. Interrupting the flow of students' speech to correct errors is demotivating. But not correcting them at all is to neglect an opportunity to help students improve their accuracy. This can be done tactfully and more anonymously at an appropriate moment later on. I have never heard a satisfactory explanation of how never correcting students improves their language ability.

All of these definitions taken together give us the characteristics of what most of us would understand by the term 'game'. However, what is perhaps more relevant for the language classroom is what teachers and students expect from the use of games in English lessons. The teacher's aims are set out in more detail below, in the design evaluation checklist, but the aims/expectations of the student will not be the same as those of the teacher. The student, on hearing the word 'game' will most likely expect an element of fun, competition and a release from any form of evaluation.

Why play games?

It is surprising how students' attitudes to exercises in school can be positively influenced by adding an element of competition to an activity and making it into a 'game'. The teacher's aims (i.e. to practise, for example, vocabulary, or a particular structure, or communication skills) remain fundamentally the same, but the student's aim has been transformed from completing the exercise to winning the game.

Doing this is very simple. But, of course, variety is the spice of life. The same format every time will lead to boredom. One approach to varying game format is to consider the two aspects: (1) participation and (2) methods of scoring.

(1) participation

Students can compete (a) as individuals, (b) in pairs, or in teams of varying sizes.

(a) Individuals can compete ...

- against themselves to see if they can complete a set task faster than on previous attempts, while still getting everything right.

- against themselves to see how much of a task they can complete within a set time frame.

- against each other to solve a set task faster than their opponent, or complete more of a set task within a given time. This can be e.g. to answer a single question, or a more complex task, e.g. to answer a series of questions.

(b) Learners can work together ...

- in pairs against other pairs to solve a task more quickly.
- in small groups to complete a task faster than the opposing team.

- in half groups/classes, taking turns to answer a question.
- as a whole class (collaborative/competitive) completing a task against the clock, then going on to see if it can beat its own record.

(2) methods of scoring

Time matters, of course. The aim can be to see how fast a whole task can be achieved, or how much of a task can be completed successfully within a set time limit.

And winning (or not losing) points also matters.

There are numerous methods of scoring, such as the traditional 'Hangman' method, where lines are drawn to show a person being hanged on a gallows.

'Sharks' is a debatably more acceptable method of scoring. Here, the aim is to avoid landing in the water and being eaten by the sharks. ☺ 'Sharks' works as follows:

- The class is divided up into two teams.
- Each team answers questions or performs tasks as required.
- The teacher reads out questions alternately to student from each team.
- Each team is represented by a figure, which starts on the top step and falls one step for each incorrectly answered question.
- The first team to land in the water with the sharks has lost. (Obviously, as the sharks will tear their limbs off them and eat them alive, causing a messy but exciting death, and prompting debate as to whether this is really more acceptable than 'Hangman'). ☺

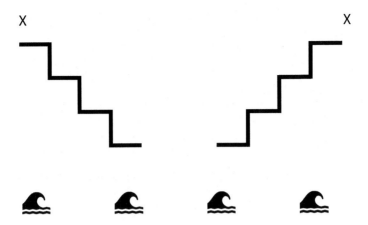

Points can be awarded to games on a varying scale, rather than on a one-to-one basis (1 point per correct answer). Very simply, here, the more questions answered correctly, the more points the student wins, as points are awarded according to a sliding (rising) scale based on the level of difficulty of the questions.

- This is an example of such a grid:

Question	Points
1	100
2	200
3	300
4	400
5	800
6	1,200
7	1,600
8	2,000
9	5,000
10	10,000

With this option, the points won for answering questions correctly cannot be lost, i.e. if the student has answered the first seven questions correctly, they have 1,600 points, and cannot lose them.

'Chains' is another method of scoring and involves an element of risk. A team that risks more can win more than a team who takes no risks, but can also lose more!

This method involves creating a 'chain' of correct answers. Each member of one team is asked a question in turn. The longer the chain of correct answers, the more points won. But! As soon as a question is answered incorrectly the chain ends and all the points are lost, unless one person has, at some point, decided to 'save' the points.

This is how 'Chains' works:

- Before each question is asked, the person whose turn it is can choose to save the points already won by their team, or to try and extend the chain by answering their question correctly.
- Saving points after each question is possible and easier, but doesn't earn many points, creating a chain of correct answers is risky and more difficult, but worth more points.

For example: The questions in the chain are worth the points in the table below.

Question	Points value (chain)
1	20
2	50
3	100
4	200
5	400
6	600
7	800
8	1000

Q1 Player 1 answers correctly, team has 20 points.
Q2 Player 2 answers correctly, team now has 50 points.
Q3 Player 3 answers correctly, team now has 100 points.
Q4 Player 4 thinks, 'I could win 200 points, but I could also lose the 100 we already have. This is getting too risky, I'll save the points.' He shouts 'save' <u>before</u> his question is asked. His team now has 100 points, the same player tries to answer his question, which is now worth 20 points, as the chain starts from the beginning again, every time points are 'saved' etc. till the team's turn (2 minutes) has finished.

- If a team manages to answer 8 questions correctly, they win 1000 points, and the chain starts again. After an equal number of rounds, the team with the most points is the winner.

'*Football*' is another method of scoring. Here is how it works:

Students are shown the following 'football field' and told that each team is kicking the 'ball' (represented by a cross/coin/counter of some sort) towards one of the goals, as in a real football match.

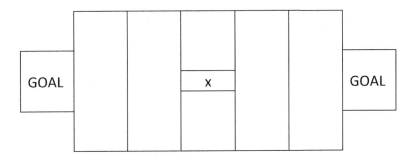

Every time a question is answered correctly, the ball is moved one square in the appropriate direction, till a team scores a goal, after which the ball is replaced in the centre and the game re-starts.

The game can also combine scoring elements of 'goals' and 'time'.

Grids with letters can also be used for scoring. These can be used in quizzes where students are required to give answers and the first letter of the answer is given.

- Teams play against each other. One member of each team competes against a member of the other team, and wins the square for their team if the answer is correct. The first square is chosen by the teacher, after that, the team which answers the question correctly is allowed to choose the next square. To win, the team has to create an unbroken line of four squares in any direction.

e.g.

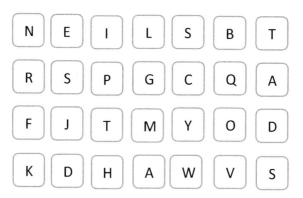

- Teams play against each other. One member of each team competes against a member of the other team, and wins the square for their team if the answer is correct. However, the team has to win all the squares in their row to win the game.

Team A L S B T N E I

Team B L C G T N S P

One team is chosen to start the game, (by, for example, tossing a coin). This team starts with the first letter in their row.

e.g. Team A starts, answers the first question correctly, the next question will begin with the second letter in their row. If Team B answers correctly fastest, the game returns to their row, and the next question will begin with the first letter in team B's row.

(This is similar to sports where you can only win a point on your own serve).

- Very simply, a question is asked for every letter in the grid. The team which has won most squares (either when the grid is full, or when time runs out) wins the game

- In this variation, the aim is simply to win more squares than the opposing team. The team that answers correctly is allowed to choose the next square at random.

In all of these variations the letters in the grid should be changed every time, to allow for different questions, and also to ensure that all the letters of the alphabet are all practised over time.

If you are not quite sure what game to choose and how to use it, the following 'game evaluation checklist' might come in useful:

Game evaluation checklist

(A) Space/time/materials

- Do I have adequate room?
- Does the game involve moving about?
- Do I have an adequate amount of time for setting things up, explaining and playing the game (including a trial run) and possibly evaluating the game afterwards?
- Do I have/will it be fairly easy to obtain enough materials for the whole class?
- Will it be necessary to duplicate materials? Also, if obtaining materials proves to be time and energy-consuming, will I be able to re-use them in future?
- Is the game suitable for the class size?

(B) Content

- What type of language input does the game contain? Is it easily comprehensible?
- Is the game culture specific? If the game is a familiar one, time may be saved in the explanation phase. Also, are there any cultural taboos which the game involves, such as asking personal questions, dealing with the subject of death?

(C) Methodological considerations

- What language aims are built into the game? Is it my aim for the students to practise/broaden their vocabulary, to practise a particular structure, or do I want them to practise communication without regard to form?
- How appropriate is the game to the learners' age? Will the learners perceive the game as childish? Is it too intellectual for them? Adults are sometimes more amenable to playing 'childish' games than teenagers.
- How appropriate is the game to the learners' linguistic ability?
  Will the game fail due to the fact that the learners are simply not able to carry out the minimum linguistic operations necessary to complete the task?
- How appropriate is the game to the learners' characters, and their perceptions of how a language is learned?
  Do the learners like playing games? Do they see them as a possible way of learning languages, or do they think that games are not a 'serious' way of learning a language?
- Are the instructions simple enough to understand? Am I going to have to spend so much time explaining the game that there is too little time left to play it, or that the proportion of explanation time to playing time does not justify the game? Will the students become demotivated due to instructions that are too difficult to understand?
- Are students used to this form of working? Will I be able to save some time at the explanation stage due to the students having played similar games before?
- Is the game competitive/non-competitive?
  Is the important element one of challenge or competition? Is the class likely to respond well to an

element of competition given its social mix? Is the level of challenge appropriate to the abilities of the class, and not so easy as to cause boredom, and not so difficult as to cause frustration?

- Sequencing: What stage of the lesson do I need the game for? Is the game for introducing material, for structured practice or free communication, i.e. at the start, in the middle or at the end of the lesson?
- Validity: Does the game actually practise what I want it to practise? If my aim is for the students to practise a particular structure, will they be able to complete the task in a different (equally valid) way, which is, however, not what I wanted to achieve?
- Learning outcomes: Does the amount of time spent justify what is being learned/practised?
- Is the game linguistically 'one-sided'? Will the students make more or less equal contributions, as far as amount and type of language produced is concerned?

(D) The role of the teacher during the game

- Do I ensure that the rules are strictly adhered to and prevent cheating?
- Am I totally impartial? Do I ensure that I, myself, don't 'cheat' by unintentionally favouring one student over another? Being totally consistent is not as easy as it might seem!
- Do I react flexibly if I see that the game is becoming 'one-sided'?
- Am I able to motivate students to keep up their interest in the game?

Games should be fun, and this is important, but it shouldn't be stuck to to the detriment of learning. As an example of this, we can take the game *'Guess the word'*, where the students are required to use only definitions with relative clauses. Strictly speaking, with many definitions it is possible to leave out the relative pronoun, as many definitions use constructions where the relative pronoun refers to the object of the sentence. The equivalent construction including the relative pronoun is equally correct, but in the interests of learning, it would make sense to insist that the relative pronoun be included in the definitions given.

General information:

Terminology: This book is aimed at learners of all ages, and covers both school students and older students. In order to keep things simple, all learners have been referred to as 'students' throughout the book.

Preparation:
- Unless otherwise stated, for all the games mentioned students will need some means of writing things down.

Distance learning:
In the same way, all the games are suitable for language learning unless otherwise described.
- Text can be displayed on the screen by the teacher.
- If students are required to work in pairs or groups, breakout rooms can be used.
- To check spelling students can write their answers into the chat.

... and now to business!

Chapter 1 Word Games

This chapter begins with a number of games incorporating the use of the alphabet. The focus is on practising and broadening the student's range of vocabulary, and being able to spell out loud in English.

1.1   Mr. 'N.'

Aim: Finding appropriate words beginning with the same letter to fit a given context
Level: Lower intermediate upwards
Duration: 10-20 minutes, depending on the time spent reading out results to class

How it works:

Students find words beginning with the same letter of the alphabet to complete a gapped text.

One day, a(n)
_____   (adjective) person called
_____   (name) left home to go and live in
_____   (country), as he had found work there as a
_____   (job).
_____   (Name) was an interesting man. He liked
_____   (verb), he adored eating
_____   (food) and drinking
_____   (drink). He drove to the airport with his
_____   (animal / bird) singing
_____   (adverb / or: type of music) on the way.

(Suggested answers for the letter 'n': nice, Neil, Norway, nurse, (Neil), negotiating, nuts, nettle juice, newt, nicely)

Task variations:

- Students use the first letter of their own first name and complete the grid.
- Students write a description using positive adjectives only.
- Students write a description using negative adjectives only.
- Students write the most ridiculous examples they can think of.
- Students write the longest/shortest examples they can think of.
- More advanced level students can be asked to find more than one word per category.
- Game is played against the clock, the student/pair/group with the most words wins, whereby there must be at least one word per category.

1.2   Word creation

Aim: Finding words using given letters (here from
                the word 'International')
Level: Any
Duration: 15 minutes upwards, depending on time
                available for task completion and checking
                answers

How it works:
'International'

Students have to find as many words as possible within a
given time limit using the letters that are contained in the
word.

- Using the letters contained in this word, you can find
  the words:
  tea, I, in, note, tin, late ….
- If the letter occurs twice, e.g. 'n' then you can use it
  twice:
  e.g. lantern
  There are at least 100 possible words!
  To get you started…

  a
  in
  ear
  nail
  Latin
  nation
  lantern

Task variations:

- Students work on their own.
- Students work in pairs (small groups).
- Students work against the clock, i.e. how many words can you find in five minutes?
- How long does it take/who is the first to find 30 words?
- Who can find the longest word?
- Who can find:
  the most words with 2/3/4/5/6 letters
  E.g.
  2 in, at, to
  3 tea, ate, ton
  4 tone, tear, rate
  5 eater, train etc
- 10 words, 2 two-letter words, 2 three-letter words, 2 four/five/six-letter words?
- the most words with 2/3/4/5/6 letters

As this activity is one which can be completed without the need for opponents, students can do it on their own while waiting to start a lesson, or at the end of a lesson.

1.3   'What word beginning with 'N' is …?'[1]

Aim: Quiz: Students compete to answer questions
                as quickly as possible (first letter of the
                answer is always given)
Level: Lower intermediate to advanced
Preparation: Teacher needs grid(s) for scoring & list(s) of
                clues (see Appendices)
Duration: 20 mins. +

How it works:

Questions: In this quiz game the letter given in the question
('What word beginning with 'N' is … ?') is the first letter of
the answer.
In answer to the question: 'What N' is … the opposite of
'day'?' the answer would, of course, be 'night'.

.

- The group is divided into two teams:
  The teacher chooses the first square and asks the first
  question. In each round, one person from each team
  (competing against each other to see who can answer
  fastest) is allowed to answer. (Next question - two
  different students and so on, till all the students have
  had a turn, then repeat from the beginning).

- The first player to give a correct answer 'wins' the
  square for the team, which is then coloured red or
  green and they are allowed to choose the next letter
  (may be any letter on the grid).

---

[1] Acknowledgement: This quiz was inspired by the TV show 'Blockbusters'

- Depending on the method of scoring, the aim is to:
  a. complete an unbroken line of four squares in a row.
  b. win more fields in the line than the opposing team.
  c. complete the line before the opposing team.
  d. win as many squares in the grid as possible.

Other rules:

- Only the designated member from each team is allowed to answer.
- They may only answer once. If they give more than one answer, their first answer stands. If their first answer is incorrect, the other team member is allowed to give one answer.
- If both answers are incorrect, another question with the same letter is asked.

Task variations:

- In addition to different methods of scoring, students can be asked to create their own clues:
  Examples:
- opposites
  What word beginning with 'N' is the opposite of 'day'?
  answer: night
- synonyms
  What word beginning with 'S' is a synonym for 'easy'?
  answer: simple
- geographical
  What word beginning with 'N' is a European country?
  answer: Norway

- historical events
  What word beginning with 'H' is a place in the South of England, after which a famous battle in 1066 was named?
  answer: Hastings
- historical figures
  Which famous historical figure, whose name began with 'H', was famous for having lots of wives?
  answer: Henry (VIII)
- fictional characters
  Which character, whose name began with 'H', lived in Baker St. and was a detective?
  answer: Holmes
- sports and hobbies
  Which game, the name of which begins with 'P', is played with a ball on a field where the players ride horses?
  answer: polo
- general knowledge
  What word beginning with 'B' is an animal that builds dams in rivers?
  answer: beaver
- descriptions
  What word beginning with 'P' is a part of some aeroplanes that spins round very quickly?
  answer: propellor
- mathematical
  What word beginning with 'T' is 18 divided by 6?
  answer: three
- superordinate terms
  What word beginning with 'B' are castle, house, bungalow and block of flats?
  answer: buildings
- subordinate terms
  What word beginning with 'B' is a type of building?
  answer: bungalow

- easy

  What word beginning with 'S' do you put on your food?

  answer: salt
- difficult

  What word beginning with 'S' is a mixture of sodium and chlorine?

  answer: salt

Further advice:

This game is suited to any of the methods of scoring in the introduction, especially the use of grids with letters mentioned above.

- In the first round, make sure each student is given a turn. After this, vary the pairings, so that each student competes against a different student every time. Levels of ability vary greatly, even within a class. If a high-ability learner is guessing against a lower achiever, then the 'playing field can be levelled' by asking a very simple question. The challenge for the student then becomes one of speed, and the weaker student will have more of a chance of winning than if it is a question of depth of knowledge.

- *Distance learning*: This game can be played using a DL platform. Squares can be easily coloured in using the Word function 'Formformat' (click on the square first). Remember that on some distance learning platforms the position of the students on the teacher's screen changes, so don't be tempted to allocate the students to teams on the basis of 'those on the left of my screen are team A' ☺. A useful idea is to get the students to add 'Team A' etc. in front of their screen names. Additionally, there may be problems with the acoustics which prevent the teacher from being able to judge accurately who answered a question correctly first, as the answers no longer come from all directions, as in the classroom, but for the same computer audio output. In such a case the students can type their answers into the chat, thus eliminating room for disagreement as to who has answered first.

1.4 'Supercalifragilisticexpialidocious[2]'

Aim: Finding long words beginning with given letters
Level: Any
Duration: 10 mins. +

How it works:

- Students (individual/pairs/small groups) try and find a word (as long as possible) beginning with each of the letters given.

- Time allowed is 2 minutes per round, no dictionaries or other aids may be used! Students get one point for each letter in each of their words, then they add up the total.

each   (4 letters = 4 points)
nice   (4)
gold   (4)
light   (5)
in   (2)
so   (2)
hieroglyphics   (13)

Total =   34 letters = 34 points

Further advice:

- Compound nouns in German are not usually one word in English. 'Schoolcarpark' (13 points) doesn't count! So it is a good idea to check at least the winning team's words at the end.

---

[2] Acknowledgement: This well-known (but meaningless) 'long word' comes from the 1964 film 'Mary Poppins'

1.5   Guessing game: Topic areas[3]

Aim: Finding as many words as possible
              connected with a given topic area within a
              given time
Level: Intermediate/advanced
Preparation: Word cards (see Appendix)
Duration: 20 minutes +
Procedure: Example – word card fruit and vegetables

How it works:

- Two teams, one pile of word field cards on the table
  between them:
- Team A picks up a card, reads the title to team B.
- Team B has one minute to name as many things they
  can think of connected with the title. Answers are
  shouted out and team A ticks off the ones that are on
  the card.
- After the minute is up, team A reads out to team B,
  'You got ...' (words that were on the list that were
  named)
  'You didn't get ...' (words that were on the list that were
  not named)
- Team B gets 1 point for each thing they named that was
  on the list.

1.	kiwi	5.	coconut
2.	pineapple	6.	pumpkin
3.	cauliflower	7.	orange
4.	potato	8.	peach

---

[3] Acknowledgement: This quiz was inspired by the game 'Outburst'.

Further advice:

When noting the items on the card that have been mentioned, instead of ticking off words on a card, students simply write the numbers 1-8 on a piece of paper and place a tick next to the number when a member of the guessing team says one of the words on the list.

- At the start of the minute, the guessing team will say so many words so quickly that the 'checking' team cannot keep up with ticking them off on the list. It is important to emphasise the honesty aspect of the game here. If team B has named a word that hasn't been ticked off, this should be corrected during the checking phase.

- For example word cards and topic areas see Appendix

Distance learning:

Students are divided into teams. The teacher sets a time limit (30 seconds per round should be enough) and gives the first team their topic area (e.g. 'parts of the body'). All the members of Team A then type as many words as they can think of into the chat. On completion of the round, the words in the chat are compared with the words on the list the teacher has made and points awarded accordingly for answers which are on the card and also correctly spelled.
The game has thus been changed from a predominantly spoken exercise to a combination of speaking and writing.
A positive side effect is that there can be no dispute about whether a particular word has been said or not, as the evidence is all there in the chat.

1.6   What on earth is it?[4]

Aim: Creating and explaining false but convincing
                definitions to fool opponents and guessing
                the meanings of obscure words
Level: Advanced
Duration: 30 minutes+

Introduction:

English has a very large vocabulary, mainly due to the fact
that there have been so many outside influences over the
centuries. Each wave of invaders brought with them their
own vocabulary, which was integrated into the language,
giving us modern day English, with its Celtic, Roman, Anglo-
Saxon, Norse and French influences, to say nothing of the
many influences from other parts of the world.
Given this fact, it is hardly surprising that there are words
which even very educated people have never seen before,
and do not know the meaning of.

How it works:

- Students form groups of three or four. Each group is
  given a word or phrase with the correct definition,
  which they mustn't show to any of the other teams.
  Their task, in their group, is to invent two or three false
  definitions.
- In turn, each group reads out its definitions to the rest
  of the class. The other groups have to guess which
  definition is the correct one. For each correctly guessed
  answer, a team gets one point. The team with the most
  points at the end is the winner.

---

[4] Acknowledgement: This quiz was inspired by the TV show 'Call My Bluff'.[4]

Example:

'Dutch courage'

- Describes the kind of false courage that is obtained by drinking alcohol before a tricky situation. *
- The name of the ship which sank with 10.000 bottles of whisky on board in the film 'Whisky Galore'.
- The name of a type of apple.

'Widgeon'

- A type of bird with reddish grey feathers, similar to a pigeon. *
- A widgeon is the name given to the large dresses worn by the ladies at court in the Middle Ages.
- A tool used in the garden for making holes to plant bulbs in.

(* = correct definition)

Possible words for explanation:

zilch	earwig
sexton	daddy long legs
pilfer	get caught short
shambles	cowslip
chough	bamboozle
flabbergasted	

For the correct definitions of these words, see Solutions

Further advice:

- It should be pointed out that the aim of the game is **not** to teach students words that they have never heard before and never will again! The language aim lies in being creative in inventing false definitions and reading them out convincingly.

- Students should be made aware that a key element of the game is being creative, and trying to convince their opponents that invented definitions are correct.
  Therefore, it is possible, to this end, to 'change' not only the grammatical form of the word, but also the pronunciation.

  For example, the word 'chough' could be variously described as a noun (true) or a verb 'to chough', or an adjective 'I'm chough'.

  The pronunciation could variously be given as, e.g.

  /tʃʌf /   (rhymes with 'rough')
  /tʃəʊ/   (rhymes with 'low')
                or
  /tʃaʊ/   (rhymes with 'how')

- The aim of the game is to fool your opponents. This can be done by creating definitions which are seemingly 'too obvious', or similar to something else.

- *Distance learning*:
  Can be played in distance learning mode - students can state whether their definition was true or false at the end of their turn, or alternatively, hold up a card saying 'true' or 'false'.

1.7   Colloquial English quiz

Aim: Broadening range of colloquial
                vocabulary
Level: Advanced
Preparation: Preparation of quiz questions as pptx or
                Kahoot quiz, or as playing cards
Duration: Quiz – 15 minutes
                group activity – open end

Introduction:

The Common European Framework of Reference for Languages (2020, p 131) in the category 'communicative language competence' states that the C1 level student should have a 'good command of idiomatic expressions and colloquialisms.' The C2 student 'should have a good command of a very broad lexical repertoire including idiomatic expressions and colloquialisms.' This is a neglected area, the focus being very often, at higher levels, on formal English, leading to the exclusion of everyday English expressions.

How it works:

- Students form pairs/teams and have a limited time to answer the questions (e.g. approx. 15 seconds per question).
- When the time is up, the winner is the team with the most correct answers.

Task variations:

- This quiz can also be played as a group or pair work activity. This variation additionally practises pronunciation (reading out loud) and listening comprehension.

- Two teams sit opposite each other with one pile of question cards between them on the table, face down.
- Team A picks up a card, reads the question and the four possible answers to the opposing team, who try and guess the answer. If they guess correctly, they win the card for their team. If not, the card is put to one side.
- Team B asks the next question, team A answers.
- The team with the most cards at the end is the winner.
- Students can be encouraged to write their own definitions:

  In groups, students receive a limited number of words, depending on the time available. They receive the correct definition and have to invent three more. Time allowing, they can either create their own presentation, for a whole class quiz, or make question cards, for playing as a pair or group work activity.

Further advice:

- If it is made clear in advance that students are not expected to know the answers, this leads to a more relaxed atmosphere.
- *Distance learning*:

  It is not possible online to play the pairs/groups variation, if the quiz is done in the 'main room', unless enough time is given for the members of the team to confer by using the private chat function. But this could be time-consuming.
- The word card variation is possible: Groups (4-6 players, i.e. two teams of 2 or 3 students) are placed in breakout rooms. Word file cards are mailed to each team (in breakout rooms) separately beforehand.
- Further materials[5]

---

[5] See: Stainthorpe, N. (2019) *As Easy as Falling Off a Log.* KDP

Colloquial English Quiz

1.   To tell a lie is to tell a '...'?

A.   sausage
B.   vealie
C.   beefie
D.   porkie

2.   To get really angry is to '...'?

A.   go spare
B.   go leftover
C.   go left
D.   go right

3.   Looking 'sheepish' means looking ...

A.   untidy
B.   stupid
C.   sleepy
D.   embarrassed

4.   If you pay more for something than it is worth, you pay 'through the ...'

A.   ears
B.   mouth
C.   nose
D.   teeth

5.   A 'Geordie' comes from ...

A.   London
B.   Newcastle
C.   Edinburgh
D.   Liverpool

---

6.   If you have guilty secrets, you have …

A.   corpses in the cellar
B.   skeletons in the cupboard
C.   bodies in the garage
D.   ghosts in the attic

7.   'If you help me, I'll help you …'
        can be expressed as '…'

A.   Each hand washes the other.
B.   You feed my cat, I'll feed yours.
C.   You need two legs to walk.
D.   You scratch my back and I'll scratch yours.

8.   Someone who is busy with lots of different
        projects at the same time has '…'

A.   a tile on every roof
B.   water in every kettle
C.   a finger in every pie
D.   a broom in every cupboard

9.   If you are really unhappy or disappointed about
        something, you are said to be 'as sick as a …'

A.   parrot
B.   donkey
C.   dog
D.   cat

10.   If you are 'caught short', you …

A.   have lost all your money.
B.   are wearing short trousers at an inappropriate time.
C.   have to go to the toilet urgently.
D.   are being mugged by a dwarf.

(For answers - see Solutions section)

1.8   Jumbled words

Aim: Re-constructing jumbled words
Level: Any
Preparation: This game is best prepared as a presentation, where each jumbled word is shown individually, followed by the solution for feedback purposes.
Duration: Variable

How it works:

- Two teams compete against each other, either the first person to shout out the correct answer winning the point (with smaller groups) or one person from each team competing against each other.

Task variations:

- additional task for beginners/intermediate students: person who guesses the word gets an additional point for spelling the word correctly out loud.
- Content:
  word fields e.g. pets, hobbies, school subjects, actions or course-book related e.g. vocabulary from chapter 1.
- missing words in context:
  e.g. Yesterday evening I went to the _____ (ameinc) with my friends (cinema)
- words with the same first letter (r)
  eard / itabbr / der
  read / rabbit / red

1.9   Get a move on!

Aim: Finding as many words as possible
                connected with a given topic area within a
                given time
Level: Any
Preparation: Stopwatch
Duration: Variable

How it works:

Students compete as a pair against other pairs. The first pair
is given a topic area (e.g. sports) and has one minute (taking
turns) to name as many as possible.

Topic area 'sports'

Teacher: 'Your topic is sports. You have one minute, starting
... now!'

Student 1   'football!'
Student 2   'golf!'
Student 1   'badminton!' ...
Student 2   etc.

                At the end of the minute the score is added
                up. The next pair competes, and so on. The
                pair with the most points at the end is the
                winner.

Further advice:

• Topic areas should be roughly of equal difficulty.

1.10 Typewriters

Aim: Practising spelling
Level: Beginners
Duration: 5-10 mins.

How it works:

- Each student is allocated a letter of the alphabet.
- The teacher says a word, the students stand up, say 'their' letter and sit down, thus spelling the word.

Task variations:

A possible variation, but with the focus on listening rather than spelling, goes like this: Each student is allocated 1 or more words (or chooses a given number of words from a list).
The teacher reads/tells a story, or plays a piece of music. Whenever the students hear 'their' words, they stand up, say 'their' word and sit down again.

Further advice:

- *Distance learning*: Can be played without any problems. Instead of standing up, students raise a hand.

1.11 Individual vocabulary quiz

Aim: Learning vocabulary
Level: Any
Duration: Flexible

There are any number of ways of learning vocabulary, and everyone has their own preferences. But I have found this one personally to be effective:

How it works:

- Take any given set of vocabulary to be learned and write it down in table format.

e.g.

L1	L2	score
Katze	cat	
Mein Hund heißt Willi.	My dog's called Willi.	
Ich habe zwei Katzen.	I've got two cats.	
etc ...	etc ...	

- The next step is to delete one column. The easiest variation would be to delete the L1 column, since most people find translating into L1 easier than into L2. Like this:

L2	L1	score
cat		
My dog's called Willi.		
I've got two cats.		
etc ...		

or, to increase the level of difficulty, delete the L2 column. Like this:

L2	L1	score
	Katze	
	Mein Hund heißt Willi.	
	Ich habe zwei Katzen.	
	etc ...	

- Print out a number of sheets, and make sure they are easily available, for times when you have a few minutes to spare.
- Try to fill in the blanks on the sheet as accurately as possible, awarding yourself a score at the end. The aim is to continually improve your score from attempt to attempt.
- Be scrupulously honest with yourself!

1.12 Crosswords

Aim: Broadening range of vocabulary
Level: Any
Duration: Variable - in general not a short activity

Crosswords need little or no explanation, and are fun to do. Playing with words is something that all of us do, and crosswords are an integral part of this process. Daily newspapers all have their regular crosswords, some easier, some more difficult. People do them on the way to work, on public transport, at work during their breaks, and when they come home from work.

Setting crosswords is a fun and relaxing way of finishing a lesson. It allows students to work at their own speed.

When setting crosswords in this way I have noted with satisfaction that, in many cases, the students were so engrossed in the activity that they failed to notice that the lesson had ended.

How it works:

You can create your own crossword puzzles very easily on www.puzzlemaker.com

These can be created and used to revise vocabulary from course book units, thus not only revising vocabulary, but also setting clues that include explanations, paraphrase, synonyms and antonyms.

Task variations:

* Students can also create their own crosswords with clues of varying levels of difficulty, and with different topic areas.

For example:

Word to be included in puzzle = 'red'

word	clue	level
red	a colour (3)	basic
red	'He was so embarrassed he went ...' (3)	intermediate
red	The company had large debts. It was in the _____. (3)	advanced

Example: Advanced (topic area: cats)

Across

1. Betray a secret: let the cat _____ (3,2,3,3)
3. A person who imitates what others do: a _____ cat (4)
5. Pretending to allow someone to have what they want, before stopping them: a cat and _____ (5,4)
6. Having a variety of options to achieve your aim: More than one way to _____ (4,1,3)
9. What curiosity did to the cat (6)
10. Got nothing to say for yourself? What's the matter - Cat _____ ? (3,4,6)
11. Short sleep (3,3)
12. Here comes Fred, as scruffy as ever! Look what the _____ ! (3,6,2)

Down

2. Agile thief who climbs up walls to get into a building: cat _____ (7)
3. Looking very satisfied, like a cat who ate all the _____ (5)
4. What mice do when the cat is not around (4)
6. Lack of space – Not enough room to _____ (5,1,3)
7. So ridiculous it would make a cat _____ (5)
8. Cause trouble: put the cat among the _____ (7)

(For answers - see Solutions section)

Further Material:[6]

---

[6] See: Stainthorpe, N. (2020) *Pigs Might Fly* . KDP

Chapter 2 Grammar Games

2.1   Lies!

Aim: All tenses: either individually, or in
                combination:
                'used to' v. present simple
                present perfect v. 'going to' future
                Modals:
                ability (can), obligation (can, must/have to)
Level: Beginners upwards
Duration: 15 mins. +

How it works:

- Individually, in pairs or small groups, students prepare
  sentences about themselves (if working individually) or
  about one of the students in their group. All of the
  sentences must be true except for one.
- Students read out their sentences to the opposing
  team, who try and guess which of the sentences is a lie.
- Scoring: Any of the options described in the
  introduction (apart from the letter grid)

Task variations:

- Sentences are created using the same tense
  e.g. present simple
  My name is Neil Stainthorpe. I <u>come</u> from the Black
  Country, in England.
- A combination of tenses to practise contrasts
  e.g. 'used to' v. present simple
  I <u>used to play</u> the trumpet, now <u>I prefer</u> reading comics.
  or:
  Up to now <u>I have always caught</u> the bus to school.
  From now on <u>I am going to</u> ...

- Time frame: sentences all refer to the past, present or future.

  e.g. past forms (various tenses)

  Yesterday at six o'clock I <u>was watching</u> Shaun the sheep.

  I <u>have</u> always <u>liked</u> learning languages.

  I <u>have been going horse riding</u> for three years now.

  Yesterday evening I was tired. I <u>had been running</u>.

- Sentences about a particular topic area

  e.g. likes/dislikes (food)

  I like honey, chocolate and lemons.

  I don't like bananas or eggs.

- Sentences with 'can' (expressing ability)

  e.g.

  I can wiggle my ears.

  I can play the ukelele.

  I can say 'hello' in 5 languages.

- Sentences with 'have to' (expressing duties, obligations)

  e.g.

  At home I have to clean my room every Saturday.

  I have to feed the cat.

  I have to unload the dishwasher.

2.2   The burglary

Aim: Giving advice
              Modal verbs - should/shouldn't have + past
              participle
              would/wouldn't have
Level: Intermediate/advanced
Duration: 25 mins. +

How it works:

- Students are presented with the situation (see 'What the police found' - Burglary - No. 27 Gorilla St.) and given two minutes to read and remember.
- The winners are those who can remember all ten items and form the corresponding advice correctly.

Situation (Example):

- While the Stainthorpes were on holiday, their house was burgled. The police went to investigate and found the following messages on the front door.
  (see below - Example)

- Can you tell the Stainthorpes what they should have done to avoid being burgled?

For example:
   They should have locked the windows.
   They should have put the ladder away.

Task variations:

- This task can also be completed using 'would have/wouldn't have' - a simplified version could be used for practising the 2nd conditional.
  e.g.

If I went on holiday, I wouldn't ...
or:
obligation with 'shouldn't'
When they go on holiday, they shouldn't ...

- Students are given two minutes to read the notes and try and remember the instructions given to each person.
  Reporting back can be done in the following way:
  e.g.
  They told/advised/asked John to ...
  or:
  They said that the workmen should ...

Example (Advanced).

What the police found: Burglary - No. 27 Gorilla St.

Dear Uncle Oswald, Thanks for getting the veg. from the farm. There is nobody home. Could you please leave it in the cellar? The front door key is under the doormat.

Dear Beryl, There is 3,000 pounds in cash in a tin on the kitchen table. It's the money we collected for the animal home. Could you take it round to them please?

Dear Fred, Thanks for lending us your new lawnmower. It's brilliant! (It must have been really expensive!) It's in the shed. You can pick it up any time. The key is under the garden gnome with the wheelbarrow.

Dear neighbours, We'll be away for the next fortnight in the Bahamas. Could you keep an eye out for burglars, please? Thanks!

Dear Tom, We forgot to take the new Bentley into the garage for its service. Would you mind? The key is in the car on the seat. Thanks!

Dear Alice, Granny brought her diamonds round for us to take to the bank for safe keeping. They're in a stocking in the dog's kennel. (Don't worry, the dog's not here!)

Dear Billy, If you need to go shopping while we're away, use the money in the vase on the mantelpiece. There's about 3,000 pounds there. Should be enough.

Dear workmen,
The lock on the back door is broken again. Could you fix it, please? Take the money from my account. My card is next to the sink. The number is 3456. Thanks!

Example (Intermediate)

Dear Uncle Oswald,
Please leave the vegetables in the cellar. We are all out.
The front door key is under the doormat.

Dear Beryl,
We collected 3,000 pounds for the animal home. It's on the kitchen table.
Could you take it to them please?

Dear Fred,
Your new expensive lawnmower is in the shed.
The key is under the garden gnome with the wheelbarrow.

Dear neighbours,
We'll be away for the next fortnight in the Bahamas. Could you keep an eye out for burglars, please? Thanks!

Dear Tom,
Can you take the new Bentley into the garage for its service? The key is in the car on the seat. Thanks!

Dear Alice,
We're looking after Granny's diamonds. They're in a stocking in the dog's kennel.

Dear Billy,
If you need to go shopping, there's 3,000 pounds in a vase on the mantelpiece.

Dear workmen,
Please fix the back door! Take the money from my account.
My card is next to the sink.
The number is 3456. Thanks!

2.3   The bank robbery[7]

Aim: Practising past simple (statements,
                questions, negation)
Level: Intermediate and above
Duration: 30 minutes +

How it works:

A.   The situation:
*   Last Friday evening sometime between 7 and 11 a bank was robbed in the city centre.
*   The police think it was you and your friend who did it!
*   You have 10 minutes to think up a story to provide yourself with an alibi!

B.   Procedure:
*   After you have prepared your story, one pair is chosen to tell us their 'story', but separately!
*   One student goes out of the room (if this is possible, otherwise the student can wear headphones). The other is asked questions by the rest of the class.
*   After 5 minutes the other person comes back into the class and is asked the same questions.
*   If there are any differences between the two versions of the story, this is taken as proof that you are guilty!

C.   Rules:
*   You did something <u>together</u>, i.e. you both went to the cinema, or you both went to the restaurant.
*   You are <u>not</u> allowed to make notes!
*   You are <u>not</u> allowed to say 'I was so drunk I can't remember!'

---

[7] Acknowledgement: This game was inspired by the popular language teaching game 'Alibis'.

2.4   Guessing the word

Aim: Practising relative clauses
Level: Intermediate and above
Duration: 15 minutes +

How it works:

- Teacher has a prepared list of words, which only he can see.
- Students are divided into teams. A member of each team is given a time limit (1-2 minutes) to explain as many words as they can (the words are given by the teacher) to the rest of the members of his team, without using the word itself. The other members of the team try to guess what the words are.
- The student has to explain the word using a relative construction, e.g. 'banana' – 'yellow fruit which grows on a tree.' Simply saying 'It's a yellow fruit' would not count.
- At the end of the time allowed, the team is given a point for every word which has been guessed correctly.
- The game continues until each member of each team has had a turn explaining.
- The winning team is the team with most points.

Further advice:

- relative pronouns which refer to the object of the sentence may be left out in normal speech.
  e.g. 'something (that) you eat for breakfast'. While this is normally perfectly acceptable English, for the purposes of this exercise, it would be better to insist students use a relative pronoun with each question. In order to ensure this happens, descriptions given

without using a relative clause don't count, even if the word is successfully guessed.

2.5   Before and after pictures

Aim: There is / there are
                prepositions
                Practising tenses, depending on the way the
                task is introduced
Level: Intermediate and above
Duration: 30 minutes +

How it works:

- Students are shown picture A with the title:

    'Yesterday I cleaned and tidied the living room.'

- and told to look at it for 1 minute and commit as many details as possible to memory.
- After 1 minute picture A is removed and picture B is shown.
- Students then have ten minutes to write down sentences describing 'What I did ...'
    e.g. I straightened the carpet ...
    etc.

Example: 'Yesterday I cleaned and tidied the living room.'

Before:

After:

Task variations:

- True / false statements (practising prepositions)

  in front of / in / under / between / on / next to / on top of

Are the following statements true or false? Students can not see the picture.

e.g.

1. There is a jigsaw puzzle on the table.
2. There is an empty coffee cup on the table.
3. The table is between the TV and the bookcase.
4. Behind the TV there are some flowers in a vase.
5. There is a cat under the sofa.
6. There are three pictures on the wall above the fireplace.
7. On the mantelpiece we can see a clock.
8. There is a lamp in front of the sofa.
9. There are some jigsaw pieces on the floor behind the TV.
10. There are some curtains in front of the bookshelves.

(For answers - see Solutions section)

- pairwork/small group exercise 'hidden objects'

One student mentally 'hides' an object in the picture. The others have to guess where it might be by asking questions.

e.g.
Is it on the carpet?
Is it behind the TV?

The same (or similar) pictures can be used for different tenses. It is simply a matter of changing the introductory sentence.

- e.g. Past perfect passive

'When I came home yesterday I saw that the living room had been cleaned and tidied.'
What had been done?

e.g.

1.   The cat had been removed.
2.   etc.

- 'Going to future'

At the moment I am watching TV. When my programme has finished, I am going to clean and tidy the living room.

e.g.

1.   I am going to get rid of the spider.
2.   etc.

2.6 Funny horoscopes[8]

Aim:	Practising 'will' future
Level:	Intermediate upwards
Duration:	30 mins. +
Preparation:	Introduce the signs of the Zodiac in English

How it works:

Horoscopes are well-known for being general, vague and applicable to almost anybody.
In this game students write two to three sentences using the 'will' future to describe their horoscope for a given date, but being as specific as possible.

e.g.

On Tuesday you will have a terrible day. On your way to school a mouse will bite you and you will fall into a hole. Your English teacher will ask you to write an essay about kangaroos.

or:

Next Monday you will be very lucky. On the way to school you will find €500 in a pink shoe outside your house. An alien will give you a lift to school in his spaceship.

Task variations:

- This game can also be used subsequently for practising reported speech:

---

[8] Acknowledgement: This activity is based on an activity from the New Cambridge Course by Swan, M. / Walter, C. (1990, p. 114).

Student 1 reads out the horoscope for a particular star sign. (see above)
Student 2 (whose star sign it is) repeats what has just been predicted:
e.g.

'Sally said I will be very lucky. She said I will find €500 in a pink shoe outside my house.'
(there is no change of tense here, because the future time frame being referred to is the same)

- One student reads out a particular sentence, the others have to try and remember which star sign it applies to.

- After the date for the horoscopes has passed, they can be compared with what actually happened.

  e.g. Last week my horoscope said a mouse would bite me. But it didn't.

- Students can also pretend that only part of the horoscope came true, and have to state which parts these were.

e.g.
Last week my horoscope said I would find €500 in a pink shoe outside my house, but I only found €400! And the shoe was green, not pink!

2.7   Pub quizzes

Aim: Practising subject/object questions with 'who', 'what' and 'how many' (with or without auxiliary 'do')
Present and past simple tenses

Level: Intermediate and above
Duration: 20 minutes +

How it works:

- Divide the class into small groups (2-4 students)
- In groups students prepare quiz questions, 3-6 per category (They must know the answers themselves.)

Examples (present simple tense):

How many legs does a spider have?
How many days are there in June?
How long does a football match usually last?
How many legs does an octopus have?
How many wheels does a tricycle have?
How many countries are there in the UK?
What do you call a bird's home?
What is the capital of Iceland?
What do you do in a mensa?
What name do we give to people who don't live in one place, but move around all the time?
What is a Jew's harp?
What animal can you see on the flag of Wales?
Who is the Austrian president?
Who plays 'Sherlock' in the TV series?
Who do you take your pet cat to when it is ill?
Who investigates crimes?

Examples (past simple tense):

Who was 'The boy who lived ...'?
Who first climbed Everest?
Who wrote 'The Lord of the Rings'?
Which Austrian actor was also Governor of California?
Who painted 'Sunflowers'?
Who sang 'We all Live in a Yellow Submarine'?

(For answers - see Solutions section)

2.8   The world's greatest liar!

Aim: Modal auxiliary 'can' to express ability
Level: Intermediate and above
Duration: 20 minutes +

How it works:

- Students write down three unbelievable 'abilities'

e.g.   I can do a handstand and juggle with my feet.
        I can swim 100 metres in 10 seconds.
        I can talk kangaroo language.

Task variations:

- Students write down one thing on a piece of paper that they can do that no-one else in the class can do e.g. I can wiggle my ears.
- Teacher collects pieces of paper, reads out the 'special abilities' and the class has to guess who is being referred to. (Strangely, this question often leads to a discussion of unusual physical abilities, much to the disgust of everybody else in the class ☺)
- Game: 'I can do more than you!'
  Along the lines of the game 'I went to market' (German 'Koffer packen') one student starts with a 'skill' ... the next student repeats the first one, then adds their own skill.
    Student 1   'I can play the piano.'
    Student 2   'I can dance and ride a horse ...'
    Student 3   'etc ...'

2.9 Our school needs changing! Now!

Aim: Modal auxiliary 'must' and 'mustn't' to
               express obligation and prohibition
Level: Intermediate and above

How it works:

- 'Things have got to change! Our school rules are old-
  fashioned and need modernising!'

Students are told that their school rules are going to be re-
written. They are going to be told what the new rules are,
and they have to try and remember as many as possible.

New School Rules

1	Teachers must all wear yellow trousers on Wednesdays.
2	Students must go to sleep in English lessons.
3	Students under the age of 12 must hop round the school.
4	If students want to borrow books from the library, they must go between midnight and 2 am. (library opening hours)
5	Students must cheat in exams.
6	Students mustn't come to school if the sun is shining.
7	Teachers must always wear odd socks.
8	Teachers must climb the stairs backwards.

- In pairs, students have 5 minutes to remember and write down as many rules as they can remember. The team that remembers most correctly is the winner.
- *Follow-up task:* Students add to the list. Any new rules must be as ridiculous as possible.

2.10   A different world – I wish, I wish ...

Aim: Practise expressing wishes
                Modals (could/would, past simple, past
                perfect)
Level: Intermediate
Duration: 20 mins +

How it works:

- Students are told to complete a wish-list of at least six sentences with their own examples according to the following pattern:

1.   I wish + would/wouldn't
     (to describe what you want other people to do/not to do/other people's annoying habits)
2.   I wish + could
     (to describe an annoying habit of your own that you would like to change)
3.   I wish + could
     (to describe an ability you would like to have)
4.   I wish/I'd rather/it's high time + past simple
     (to describe how you would like things to be/or not to be)
5.   I wish + past perfect
     (to describe how things you would have liked things to happen differently)
6.   I hope (for future wishes)

Example:

How I would like things to be!

I wish people wouldn't block the supermarket aisle with their trolleys when they stop to look for something.
I wish I could stop dropping things everywhere!
I wish I could yodel.
I wish my parents were millionaires.
I wish we didn't have swimming lessons on Monday mornings. (negative)
It's high time the canteen started serving chips!
I wish my parents hadn't given my sticker collection away!
I hope the summer never ends!

- The teacher collects in the pieces of paper, reads out the lists of wishes and students have to try and guess who wrote them.

Chapter 3 Communication Games

3.1   I'm the expert![9]

Aim: Communication: Talking about an
                          area of special interest
Level: Intermediate/advanced
Duration: 30 minutes+ (depending on group
                          size, time allowed for discussion,
                          degree of reporting back)

How it works:

- Each student chooses a topic area which they think they
  know a little more about than the other people in the
  class.
- Part 1: (if you are being interviewed)
  Be prepared to talk and answer questions on your own
  topic (for about 5 minutes).
- Part 2: (if you are the interviewer)
  Be prepared to report back to the rest of the class about
  what you have learned.

Further advice:

When this idea is suggested, most students are usually
horrified and insist that they aren't experts on anything, but
they just need to be told that it has to be a topic which they
know a little bit about. It could be anything from a particular
hobby, to knowing about hamsters or how to bake
something, how to play the ukelele or being an expert on
Mary Poppins. It is often surprising the things you and the
students find out about each other!

---

[9] Acknowledgement: This activity is based on the popular EFL activity often known as
'The Expert Game'.

Task variations:

Students can be allocated topics to talk about. Examples could be:
- a game you like playing
- something you'd like to have
- my favourite book
- a really awful film
- things that make me laugh
- my pet hates
- my plans for next weekend
- my worst holiday ever

If so desired, it is possible to a certain extent to focus on particular grammatical forms.

e.g.
- my pet hates (pres. simple)
- my worst holiday ever (past tenses)

3.2   Keep talking![10]

Aim: Communication: practising sustained
                         monologues: talking about an area of
                         special interest
Level: Intermediate/advanced
Duration: Variable depending on the number of
                         rounds played

How it works:

- Students are given a random topic and asked to speak about it for 60 seconds without hesitating, repeating themselves (with the exception of the name of the topic itself) or going off topic (saying anything irrelevant).
- Player 1 starts talking and attempts to keep going for a minute.
- Other players shout 'stop', if they think the speaker has broken one of the three rules mentioned above.
- If the challenge is successful, the challenger continues talking on the same topic.
- The round continues as before until the minute is finished. A new topic is chosen for the next round.
- The game is over when all the rounds have been played. The winner is the participant with the most points.

Points are awarded as follows:

- 1 point for a successful challenge (to the challenger)
- 1 point for the current speaker if the referee thinks a challenge is unjustified
- 2 points for whoever is speaking when the minute ends

---

[10] Acknowledgement: This activity is based on the radio show 'Just a Minute'

Possible topic areas: (Example)
pets, school, free time, my favourite place, my favourite TV programme, computers, zoos, my favourite school subject, my last holiday etc.

Task variations:

- If the task is too difficult to do spontaneously, students can be given time to prepare topic areas.

Distance learning:

Problems with acoustics and time lag caused by slow internet connections could make this difficult to do as a distance learning activity.

3.3   Spot the differences

Aim: Picture description / present simple
Level: Intermediate and above
Duration: 20 minutes+

How it works:

- In pairs, students have to find the differences between the two pictures. They are not allowed to look at their partner's picture, so the differences have to be found by describing their picture to their partner.
- Scoring: this exercise can be done against the clock, i.e. 'Who can find the most differences in 10 minutes?' but also by allowing all the students to continue until at least one pair has found a specified number of differences.

Task variations:

The task can be made easier by pre-teaching/revising certain vocabulary items:

- All of the pre-taught items are useful for finding differences:
  e.g. garden gnome, wheelbarrow, spade, ladder, barrel
    or:
- (more difficult) Some of the pre-taught vocabulary items might help in finding the differences, others might be irrelevant.
    e.g. garden gnome, bicycle, wheelbarrow, shoes, spade, aeroplane, ladder, climbing frame, barrel, guitar, pot of honey ...

Picture A

Picture B

(For answers - see Solutions section)

3.4   Picture dictation

Aim: Listening comprehension
Level: Any
Preparation: Paper and crayons/felt pens
Duration: 15 minutes +

How it works:

- One student reads a short text, the others simply have to draw what he/she describes. On a simple level, it might go like this:
  'In my picture there is a large house with a red door, four windows, with green curtains and smoke coming out of the chimney.
  On the left hand side of the house there is an apple tree with red apples and on the right a garage with a small car in it.'
  etc ...
- When the students have finished, they can compare pictures with their neighbours.
- The pictures can then be described back to the 'describer'.

Task variations:

Students are instructed to deliberately 'mis-draw' one aspect of the picture. When the pictures are finished, the students can try and describe what is wrong in each other's pictures.

Distance learning:

Students who volunteer can be allowed to share their drawing on the screen and describe it to the class.

3.5   A tall story

Aim: Listening/reading comprehension, correcting
              factual errors
Level: Intermediate and above
Duration: 30 mins. +

How it works:

This activity can be done either as a listening or reading
comprehension exercise.
Pairs/groups of students compete to see who can identify
and correct as many errors as possible within a given time
limit.

Introduction:

Mr. Motormouth loves Britain. And English. But,
unfortunately, he doesn't always get his facts right. In fact,
to be honest, he hardly ever gets it right. But that doesn't
stop him telling everybody about it at great length!
Can you help him to get it right for once?

• Reading exercise:

Students are given the text and the time limit includes
reading the test and finding the errors.

Christmas in Great Britain

There are 12 errors in this text. Can you find and correct them?

'Hi! Today I want to tell you about Christmas in Great Britain. People are very fond of Christmas cards, in fact they start sending them to each other in August. Santa Claus brings them in his sleigh, pulled by Rudolf, the red-nosed unicorn, and throws them down the chimney.

English people love singing Christmas songs called 'Christmas Susies'. One of the best known is 'We wish you a Happy Christmas'.

Sometimes people hang up a plant called 'mistlehand' as a decoration, and tradition has it that if you meet someone directly underneath it, you should shake their hand.

The big celebration for the family is on the 24th of December, called 'Christmas lunch', where they traditionally eat fish and chips, followed by the traditional banana yoghurt.'

(For answers - see Solutions section)

Task variations:

- Reading can be done together (and vocabulary explained) before starting the clock.
- Listening exercise: Teacher reads text twice before starting the clock.
- Students are told exactly how many mistakes are in the text.
- Additional activity: Students prepare questions on corrected texts. Class is divided into two teams, who alternate asking and answering questions. Points are awarded for correct answers (may also be awarded for correctly formulated questions).

Chapter 4 Pronunciation Games

4.1   Who am I?

Aim: Practising intonation, pronunciation as a
            means of expressing emotions
Level: Any
Duration: 10 mins. +

How it works:

- Take a dialogue. Prepare a list of characters with names
  such as:
            Mr. Happy
            Ms. Sad
            Mr. Fast
            Ms. Slow
            Mr. Loud
            Ms. Quiet
            etc.

- Students work in pairs: Read dialogue in the manner of
  their chosen character.
- Partner has to guess which character they have chosen.
- Choose a different role and repeat.

4.2   Word chains

Aim: Recognising final sounds in words
Level: Any
Duration: 5 minutes +

How it works:

- Students make a word 'chain'. P1 starts with a word,
  student 2 gives a word beginning with the final sound of
  the first student's word. e.g.
    P1   cat
    P2   train
    P3   nose
    P4   zoo etc.

This game is very simple, so variation in the scoring system
is to be recommended.

Task variations:

- Against the clock. How long does it take to go round the
  class with every student participating?
  (If such a round is repeated, then make sure that the
  words used are new ones, otherwise this distorts the
  result.)
- Against each other, in pairs, small groups – however you
  decide to divide the students up.

4.3   What's the same?

Aim: Sound recognition
Level: Advanced
Duration: 20 mins +

How it works:

- Teacher reads out the words in list below. Students have to 'hear' which sound is the same in all of the words.

Which sound can you hear in all these words?

1.	cold	window	ago	slow	/əʊ/
2.	inside	nice	library	like	/aɪ/
3.	down	nice	cinema	kitchen	/n/
4.	age	gin	juice	jeep	/dʒ/
5.	author	farmer	contain	tomato	/ə/
6.	village	view	live	give	/v/
7.	blog	gale	degree	grassy	/g/
8.	zoo	flows	fans	zoom	/z/
9.	Greece	geese	eats	shouts	/s/
10.	tooth	thing	three	north	/θ/
11.	them	this	these	breathe	/ð/

Task variations:

This can also be done as a reading exercise.

4.4   Odd one out

Aim: Sound recognition
Level: Advanced
Duration: 20 mins+

How it works:

- Teacher reads out the words in list below. Students have to 'hear' the word which doesn't have the same sound as the others.
- In each group of words there is one word which doesn't have the same sound as the other four in the group. Which word is it?
  Which sound can you hear in all the other four words in the group?

1.	extreme	degree	suit	ceiling	ensuite
2.	guidance	identical	site	virtual	finance
3.	front	tune	instructor	run	tunnel
4.	curtain	early	fear	first	prefer
5.	road	court	audience	broad	form
6.	again	container	computer	about	comb
7.	comb	overall	through	won't	though
8.	scare	pair	fear	pear	dare
9.	ear	steer	bear	weird	pier
10.	lower	doubt	cow	shower	plough
11.	threw	sue	sew	through	moo
12.	park	laugh	master	mast	park
13.	cake	weigh	height	stay	change

(For answers - see Solutions section)

4.5   My teacher needs help!

Aim: Listening for mistakes, pronunciation
                practice
Level: Any
Duration: 5 mins. +

How it works:

- Teacher reads any text, students have to listen carefully
  and shout 'Stop!', every time the teacher makes a
  deliberate mistake. The aim is not only to practise
  listening for detail, but also pronunciation.
- The teacher deliberately misreads words which are
  commonly mispronounced and asks for the correct
  version. With a bit of imagination, this can be made to
  sound amusing.

Example:

'One day, little Billy was feeling very <u>happy</u>! His <u>father</u> saw
him and ...'
Teacher reads:
'One day, little Billy was feeling very <u>yellow</u>!' (students shout
'Stop!' and provide the word 'happy'.) The teacher
continues reading, 'His <u>crocodile</u> saw him and ...'

'Yellow' and 'crocodile' are a means of eliciting the (often
mispronounced) words 'happy' and 'father'.

Criteria for missing out words:
- words which contain difficult sounds:
  e.g. job   /dʒ/
       father /ð/
       village /v/
       cat   /æ/
       for   /ɔ:/

- words which are used in German but pronounced with different sounds:
  e.g. job, happy
- words which have close German equivalents, but are stressed differently in German:
  e.g. 'pullover, 'elephant 'cousin, 'orange, 'telephone etc.
- Instead of leaving out single words, longer phrases can be left out to practise:
- weak forms
  e.g. piece of cake, it's for me, she's from England ... etc.
- linking
  e.g. two of them etc.
- intonation
  e.g. I love apples!

4.6   Phonemic word searches[11]

Word searches are, of course, a common and popular type
of puzzle. One possible variation is to create a word search
using the IPA (International Phonetic Alphabet), found in
dictionaries and course books as an aid to pronunciation.

Aim: Practising use of the IPA
Level: Advanced for phonemic word search, lower
                intermediate and above for other types
Duration: (A word of warning here – word searches
                can be time-consuming. Suitable for times
                when you have lots of time to spare!)

How it works: (See example below)

- Students have to find, in this case, the names of ten
  animals in the grid, horizontally, vertically (but not
  diagonally) and either from left to right or right to left.

Animals
(The transcription of these words does not include
the rhotic 'r' given in superscript in standard
dictionary transcriptions)

---

[11] Acknowledgement: The phonemic word search is based on an activity in Hewings, M.
(2007, p. 131) *English Pronunciation in Use*. CUP.

Can you find the names of fourteen animals in the grid?

k	d	əʊ	k	e	t	tʃ	r	e	h
eɪ	ɔɪ	m	aʊ	s	ʊ	ʌ	æ	dʒ	e
n	r	ə	s	ə	t	ɔ:	t	ə	dʒ
s	ɑ:	s	t	aʊ	dʒ	æ	ʌ	p	h
h	t	eə	æ	m	ɪ	r	ʃ	k	ɒ
ʌ	æ	b	ʊ	b	b	ɔ:	l	e	g
s	k	n	ʃ	h	æ	m	s	t	ə
b	aɪ	g	ə	lə	t	aʊ	p	ʊ	ʃ
b	æ	dʒ	æ	t	aɪ	g	ə	r	e
k	ɔ:	r	dʒ	æ	ʃ	u	g	ɒ	d

Task variations:

The level of difficulty can be adapted as follows:
- Can you find these (English) words in the square?
- Can you find the English equivalent of these (German) words in the square?
- Can you find 10 words in the square connected with the topic of animals?
- How many words can you find in the square connected with ... (e.g. animals)?
- Students are limited by time.
- A different activity completely would be to give students a blank grid and let them make word searches for each other.

e.g. Create a word search grid containing:

ten verbs / colours / ten nouns / adjectives / ten things you would find in the classroom/ living room, etc.

You can create your own word searches very easily at www.puzzlemaker.com

4.7 Phonemic word maze[12]

Aim:	Identifying voiced and voiceless plural/3rd person 's'
Level:	Beginners upwards
Duration:	15 mins+

How it works:

• Students need to find their way through the maze from START to FINISH moving one space horizontally or vertically (but not diagonally). They may only use spaces where the word ends with a voiced plural or 3rd person 's'.

(Whether the final sound is voiced depends on the sound preceding it. A plural 's' after /t/ will be voiceless, since the /t/ is also voiceless.)

START						
mails	eats	chants	parents	dies	animals	runs
dogs	friends	boys	nights	goats	tricks	hats
cats	rocks	holidays	tents	bikes	cooks	streets
books	it's	girls	helps	necks	potions	fits
answers	worms	learns	bagpipes	days	brooms	learned
apples	bakes	nuts	risks	times	bikes	sounds
hands	days	sits	talks	trees	hats	has
hits	babies	goes	takes	roses	toilets	heads
creatures	sits	colours	prizes	arms	bats	cabs
						FINISH

Task variations:

Students have to find their way through the maze by identifying squares containing:

---

[12] Acknowledgement: The above phonemic word maze is based on an activity in Bowen, T. & Marks, J. (1992) *The Pronunciation Book.* Longman.

- voiced plural 's'
- plural /iz/'
- voiced 'th'
- voiceless 'th'
- words containing a silent letter (e.g. 'climb')

(For answers - see Solutions section)

4.8   Dramatic dialogues?

Aim: Pronunciation practice expressing various
                emotions using dialogues
Level: Intermediate and above
Duration: 10 mins. +

How it works:

Read the dialogue out loud, making sure the way the students read it reflects the 'speaking verb' given.

- Example: The Haunted Castle

The others heard <u>an enthusiastic shout</u>:
'Look! A haunted castle! Let's go in and frighten the ghosts!'
It was Paul, the American language teacher.
Edith wasn't so sure. She said <u>hesitantly</u>, 'It looks creepy to me,'
'I'm not scared of ghosts,' Gudrun said <u>unconvincingly</u>.
Paul said <u>confidently</u>, 'I'd like to see the ghost that could scare me!'
Lisi didn't notice what was going on around her, and said <u>happily,</u> 'It's my cat's birthday today! Let's celebrate!'
Fred said <u>angrily</u>, 'No! We're here in London to learn something today. Here's the modern art gallery. It's called 'The Modern Crate'.'
'That's because it used to be a brewery,' Grandad said, <u>sounding like a 90 year-old.</u>
Sally said, <u>far too loudly</u>, 'Grandad is sooooo clever!'
'He should be a teacher!' Paul <u>whispered</u>.
Did I hear someone say 'brewery?' <u>said Harry excitedly</u>.
'I think modern art is <u>USELESS</u>!' said Gudrun.
'Well, I don't. I <u>LOVE</u> it!' replied Doris! Let's go!

Task variations:

Students can adapt dialogues from the coursebook by changing the speaking verbs, adding adverbs, either of their own choice, or from a list provided by the teacher.
Possible speaking verbs:

- say
- whisper
- shout
- joked
- begged
- insisted

Possible adverbs:

Fred said:
- happily
- sadly
- slowly
- quickly
- quietly
- loudly
- angrily
- nervously
- hesitantly
- rudely
- politely

4.9　Spot the word

Aim:　　　　To revise pronunciation of words, awareness
　　　　　　of different L1/L2 pronunciation
Level:　　　Beginners
Duration:　5-10 mins.

How it works:

- Students are given a picture with relevant vocabulary. (This can be one picture of e.g. a classroom scene, or flashcards of several different items.) All the students can see the picture(s).
- Familiarisation:
  1. Teacher gives students the first sound of one of the words. e.g. 'No. 1 – /e/...'
  2. Students shout out the word 'elephant'
     (This exercise can draw attention to the difference in pronunciation between English and German 'elephant' v 'Elefant'.)
- All students then repeat correct pronunciation of the word.
- Game: Students are divided into pairs/teams. Teacher reads first sound and the first student to shout out the correct answer wins a point for the correct word and a point for the correct answer.

Possible word categories:

- words where the first sound is identical in both languages, e.g.

s	school	m	mouse
	sandwich	d	door

- words which begin with sounds which may be difficult for German learners, e.g.

w	wheel	a	astronaut, apple
v	volleyball	j	jam
p	pig		

- words which start with a letter that is pronounced in a completely irregular way, e.g.

a	agent	e	eleven
		o	oven

Chapter 5 Young learners and beginners

General considerations

A distinction has to be made between young learners and beginners. Young learners who are, say, in their first year at primary school (aged 6) learn under different conditions to older 'beginners', say, aged 11-12, or older still.

Young learners bring with them to class a general curiosity about the world, a love of play, a lack of teenage inhibitions and very often an excellent memory for pictures. (Most people who have played Kim's game (sometimes called Pelmanisms, or in German (strangely) 'Memory') will confirm a feeling of surprise at the way young children can remember the position of picture card pairs!). Older children and adult beginners, on the other hand, may display a greater degree of inhibition on the one hand but a greater ability to approach new content from a cognitive perspective, coupled with a longer attention span and less desire/need to be physically active.
So what does this mean in practice?

A learner beginning primary school at this age may know how to count up to ten in English, but not be able to name numbers out of sequence, as the numbers have been learned simply as a rhyme.

There is no point in trying to explain grammar rules cognitively. Additionally, the written word takes a back seat, preference being given to visual aids.

On the other hand, as English is taught to a considerable extent in the form of games, rhymes and songs, it is rare to find a primary child who does not enjoy English lessons in school. The pressure of tests and exams is non-existent.

Pronunciation is an area where, potentially, considerable progress may be made compared with older beginners. The 'Critical Age Hypothesis' (Lenneberg, 1967) states that children have, up to the age of about 14, a natural aptitude for acquiring pronunciation, after which it is virtually impossible to acquire a native-like pronunciation any more. Young children are far less inhibited when it comes to singing, repeating what the teacher says, and imitating 'silly' voices, for example. There are none of the inhibitions and shyness present in teenagers.

(A word of warning here: It may not be effective to tell a child aged six to put the tip of their tongue underneath their front teeth so as to pronounce /θ/ in 'three' correctly, as children that age are very often in the process of losing their milk teeth ☺).

Repetition can be a strong motivational factor with young learners, especially if done in a playful way. Once again, variation is paramount here. There is nothing worse than half-hearted repetition, especially if the teacher gets the children to repeat simultaneously and not consecutively, and doesn't insist on all the children taking part.

Repeating consecutively (after the teacher, as opposed to with), means the teacher can focus on listening to the students and correct any errors.

So, how can we vary repetition?
We can use the folllowing table as a guide to possible variations:

Who?	E.g. • single students, front row, back row boys, girls repeat together • individual students, consecutively
What?	• students repeat the same or different things
How much?	• repeat single words, a phrase, a whole sentence
How?	• words and phrases can be repeated quietly, loudly, quickly, slowly, with varying intonation, and with varying emotions

5.1 Vocabulary maths

Aim: Practising numbers, elementary maths,
              reading
Level: Beginners
Duration: 20 mins +

How it works:

- Teacher uses list with numbers and words or numbers and pictures to ask elementary maths questions.
- Example: Topic area – food / colours / animals

1	eggs	11	pizza	21	bear
2	football	12	goldfish	22	chips
3	cat	13	white	23	muffins
4	dog	14	milk	24	tea
5	honey	15	black	25	cheese
6	green	16	sugar	26	apples
7	chocolate	17	rabbit	27	bananas
8	pink	18	juice	28	red
9	blue	19	bread	29	blue
10	hamster	20	yellow	30	carrots

Question: What is 4 plus 8?
(Student calculates 4 + 8, arrives (hopefully) at the answer 12 and gives the correct answer – 'goldfish'. The student wins a point for their team.)

- Scoring system: Football (see introduction), but any of the above mentioned is applicable. Teacher can play two 'halves' of 5 minutes each.
- *Distance learning*: Students type answers into the chat.

Task variations:

- subtraction: What is 30 minus 10?   yellow
- division: What is 30 divided by 6?   honey
- multiplication: What is 3 times 5?   black

- increased number of items:
  e.g. (teacher) 'What is 5 plus 2 plus 3 plus 6?'
  students answer (shout out)   'bread'

- use of 'minus', 'divided by' and 'times' in various
  combinations:
  e.g. (teacher) 'What is 5 minus 2 plus hamster?'
  students answer (shout out)   'white'

- asking (the whole range of) questions not with
  numbers, but with words:
  e.g. (teacher) 'What is apples plus eggs?'
  students answer (shout out)   'bananas'

Further advice:

When introducing the game, students can be asked to guess
how it works, by giving examples with the answers:
e.g.
- number plus number
  e.g. 1 plus 3 is dog
- number + word (students answer with word)
  e.g. 10 plus chocolate is rabbit
- word + word
  e.g. cat plus dog is chocolate

5.2   Disappearing words or phrases

Aim: Practising vocabulary
Level: Beginners
Duration: 10 mins. +

How it works:

- Items of vocabulary to be practised are placed next to word cards, or simply in an easily recognisable pattern. E.g. ten items of vocabulary are placed next to each other on the board and a student asked to simply read out the list.

Task variations:

- Combination of word and picture cards: Word cards and picture cards are placed next to each other to form two columns. A student is chosen (or volunteers) to read out the list.
- Once the list has been successfully read, with adequate repetition, and according to the principles of 'who, how, how much and what' (see above) one of the word cards is removed, leaving a gap.
- The list has to be read again, including the picture for which there is no word card.
- This process is repeated until all the word cards have 'disappeared'. The challenge grows from round to round. The advantages of this exercise are firstly, that the vocabulary is repeated (and heard) at least ten times, but in a challenging, competitive way – 'Can you read the whole list without making a mistake?'
- With younger learners where the use of word cards is inappropriate, picture cards can be placed in a 3 x 3 pattern, forming a square. This makes varying the 'What' very simple:

Students can be asked to read:

- row 1, 2 or 3
- column 1, 2 or 3
- diagonally from bottom left to top right, or from bottom right to top left
- an increasing number of items pointed to in random order by the teacher (a sort of progressive memory task)

Further advice:

The teacher can differentiate here by deliberately asking weaker students to contribute while the list is still relatively complete, thus giving them a feeling of achievement.
Conversely, the higher achievers can be asked towards the end of the exercise, to give them the opportunity to complete a more demanding task.

5.3   Last one standing?

Aim: Practising counting/the alphabet
Level: Beginners
Duration: 5 mins +

How it works:

- Students stand up. In turn, they count in sequence:
  P1   '1',
  P2   '2'
  P3   '3' ...
  and so on, according to the range of numbers being practised.
- But every time e.g no. '5' is reached, the student has to sit down. When the range of numbers being practised (e.g. 1-20) is completed, the students simply carry on counting, starting from 1 again.
- The winner is the student who is left standing at the end.

Task variations:

- The number of the student who has to sit down is changed after every complete game. Also, to speed up the game, more than one number can be chosen, i.e. '3' and '7', or '5', '10' and '15'.
- This game can be used to practise the alphabet. Substitute letters for numbers. e.g. 'E' 'J' 'O' and 'T' sit down.
- Choose the letters of a name. e.g. 'N', 'E', 'I' and 'L' sit down.

Distance learning:

This game is not easy to play in distance learning form.

5.4   Guess how old I am!

Aims: This activity only requires a couple of basic
               phrases to do, and is therefore short, but
               fun to do
Level: Any
Duration: 5 mins +

How it works:

- Student writes down the name of a famous person
  and his/her age, which must be between 1 and 63, but
  doesn't tell the teacher the age.
- Teacher: 'What's your name?'
- Student: 'Mickey Mouse'
- Teacher: 'Tell me: Can you see your age in these
              boxes? In which ones?'
- Student: 'In box 1, 3 and 6.'
- Teacher: 'Ok ... (pauses to let telepathic skills work ... ☺)
              'Then you are 41 years old!'

Task variations:

- Teacher hands out pre-prepared cards with pictures of
  cartoon characters on them with 'name' and a blank
  space next to 'age' on them. Students fill in the 'age' of
  their character.
- (Procedure as above) Teacher informs student: 'You are
  ___ years old.'
- How it works:
  Student's character is e.g. 47. The age is therefore visible
  in boxes 1, 3, 4, 5 and 6. The teacher adds up the very
  first number of every box the student mentions, giving
  the age – in this case *32+8+4+2+1 = 47.*

- Suspense: The teacher can announce the age of each character in turn, or wait until everyone has finished, then read out the whole list:
E.g.   Superman is 10 years old. Alice in Wonderland is 42 years old. Shaun the sheep is 18 years old. And so on.

- Students find out the age of a famous person (procedure as above)

Further advice:

This activity can be incorporated into other activities
E.g. a common activity at young learner level is drawing monsters as a means of practising the topic area 'parts of the body'. The monster can be given an 'age' as well.

Magic number table:

1	2	3
32 33 34 35	16 17 18 19	08 09 10 11
36 37 38 39	20 21 22 23	12 13 14 15
40 41 42 43	24 25 26 27	24 25 26 27
44 45 46 47	28 29 30 31	28 29 30 31
48 49 50 51	48 49 50 51	40 41 42 43
52 53 54 55	52 53 54 55	44 45 46 47
56 57 58 59	56 57 58 59	56 57 58 59
60 61 62 63	60 61 62 63	60 61 62 63

4	5	6
04 05 06 07	02 03 06 07	01 03 05 07
12 13 14 15	10 11 14 15	09 11 13 15
20 21 22 23	18 19 22 23	17 19 21 23
28 29 30 31	26 27 30 31	25 27 29 31
36 37 38 39	34 35 38 39	33 35 37 39
44 45 46 47	42 43 46 47	41 43 45 47
52 53 54 55	50 51 54 55	49 51 53 55
60 61 62 63	58 59 62 63	57 59 61 63

5.5 Fizz buzz

Aim: Practising counting/the alphabet
Level: Beginners upwards, depending on the age
             of the students
Duration: 5 mins +

How it works:

- Another counting game. This time the words 'fizz' and 'buzz' replace pre-defined numbers.
  e.g.
  'fizz' = 3,
      = any number containing a 3 (3, 13, 23 etc.)
      = any number which can be divided by 3 (3, 6, 9, etc.)
  'buzz' = 5,
      = any number containing a 5 (5, 15, 25 etc.)
      = any number which can be divided by 5 (5, 10, 15, etc.)
- Careful! 15 is 'fizz buzz', 33 is 'fizz fizz', 35 is 'fizz buzz'
- Students count in turn, whoever makes a mistake is out.

Task variations:

This game should be played quickly and needs a lot of concentration! It is probably easiest to begin with 'fizz' only. The prerequisite is that the students have already learned their 'times tables'.

- The simple version 'fizz' would go as follows:

1	=	1	9	=	fizz	17	=	17
2	=	2	10	=	10	18	=	fizz
3	=	fizz	11	=	11	19	=	19
4	=	4	12	=	fizz	20	=	20
5	=	5	13	=	fizz	21	=	fizz
6	=	fizz	14	=	14	22	=	22
7	=	7	15	=	fizz	23	=	fizz
8	=	8	16	=	16	24	=	24 ...

For younger children version 1 ('fizz') is probably demanding enough. But more difficult versions can be played with older students.

- The harder version ('fizz buzz') would go like this:

1	=	1	9	=	fizz	17	=	17
2	=	2	10	=	buzz	18	=	fizz
3	=	fizz	11	=	11	19	=	19
4	=	4	12	=	fizz	20	=	buzz
5	=	buzz	13	=	fizz	21	=	fizz
6	=	fizz	14	=	14	22	=	22
7	=	7	15	=	fizz buzz	23	=	fizz
8	=	8	16	=	16	24	=	fizz...

- Another variation: Students can count down from a given number.

Chapter 6 Number puzzles

6.1   Looks familiar?

Aim: Practising numbers, elementary maths,
                reading
Level: Beginners
Duration: 10 mins. +

How it works:

- Calculate the following, step by step, using a pen and
  paper. The results might be surprising!

    1. Choose any number between 1 and 7.
    2. Multiply it by 2. Add 5. Multiply it by 50.
    3. If you've had your birthday already this year, add
        1771.
    4. If not, then add 1770.
    5. Subtract the year when you were born.

    You should have a three digit answer:

Does anything look familiar about your final number?

(For answers - see Solutions section)

Further advice:

This puzzle works with these numbers for the year 2021.
From 2022 onwards, clues 3 and 4 should read as follows:
        3.   ... add 1772
        4.   ... add 1771

From 2023 onwards, clues 3 and 4 should read as follows:
        3.   ... add 1773
        4.   ... add 1772

6.2   Telepathy

Aim: Practising numbers, elementary maths,
             reading
Level: Beginners
Duration: 10 mins. +

How it works:

Teacher:
- 'Follow the steps below, then I will tell you what you are thinking of!
- Choose a number between 1 and 9.
- Multiply by 9
- You should have a 2-digit number. Add the 2 digits together.
- Subtract 5
- Think of your number as a letter of the alphabet
  1=A, 2=B, 3=C etc.
- Think of a European country (in English!) beginning with your letter.
- Now take the second letter of your country and think of an animal beginning with that letter.
- Now think of the colour of that animal.'
- Now ask your students, 'Who is thinking of a grey elephant in Denmark?' and wait for the gasps of surprise and amazement at your telepathic abilities.

(About half the class will answer 'yes!', a quarter will be thinking of a brown eagle in Denmark, once in a while someone will mention a grey eel and the remaining 25% will have got their sums wrong. ☺)

6.3   All the same ...

Aim: Practising numbers, elementary maths,
              reading
Level: Beginners
Duration: 10 mins. +

How it works:

- Choose a number
- Add 9
- Double the answer
- Add 3
- Multiply by 3
- Subtract 3
- Divide by 6
- Subtract the original number

(For answers - see Solutions section)

Solutions

1.6   What on earth is it?

word:	meaning:
zilch	absolutely nothing!
earwig	brown insect
sexton	person who digs graves
daddy long legs	insect with very long legs
pilfer	steal
get caught short	have to go to the toilet
shambles	chaos
cowslip	small flower
chough	bird
bamboozle	to fool sb.
flabbergasted	amazed

1.7   Colloquial English Quiz

1.	D	a porkie
2.	A	go spare
3.	D	look embarrassed
4.	C	pay through the nose
5.	B	Newcastle
6.	B	skeletons in the cupboard
7.	D	You scratch my back, I'll scratch yours.
8.	C	have a finger in every pie
9.	A	as sick as a parrot
10.	C	have to go to the toilet

1.12 Crosswords

Across

1. out of the bag
3. copy
5. mouse game
6. skin a cat
9. killed
10. got your tongue
11. cat nap
12. cat dragged in

Down

2. burglar
3. cream
4. play
6. swing a cat
7. laugh
8. pigeons

2.5 Before and after pictures

'Yesterday I cleaned and tidied the living room.'

1. I removed the spider and the cobwebs.
2. I watered the plant.
3. I turned off the TV.
4. I finished the jigsaw.
5. I threw the cat out.
6. I straightened the carpet.
7. I lit the fire.
8. I took the dirty dishes into the kitchen.
9. I took the mirror above the fire down and put up a picture of granny.
10. I pulled back and tied the curtains.

True / false statements

1.	T	6.	F
2.	F	7.	T
3.	T	8.	F
4.	T	9.	F
5.	F	10.	T

2.7   Pub Quizzes

- How many legs does a spider have?
  eight
- How many days are there in June?
  Thirty
- How long does a football match usually last?
  ninety minutes
- How many legs does an octopus have?
  eight
- How many wheels does a tricycle have?
  three
- How many countries are there in the UK?
  four
- What do you call a bird's home?
  nest
- What is the capital of Iceland?
  Reykjavik
- What do you do in a mensa?
  eat food
- What name do we give to people who don't live in one place, but move around all the time?
  nomads
- What is a Jew's harp?
  a musical instrument
- What animal can you see on the flag of Wales?
  a dragon
- Who is the Austrian president?
  Alexander van der Bellen (in 2021)
- Who plays 'Sherlock' in the TV series?
  Benedict Cumberbatch
- Who do you take your pet cat to when it is ill?
  the vet
- Who investigates crimes?
  a detective

- Who was 'The boy who lived ...'?
  Harry Potter
- Who first climbed Everest?
  Edmund Hillary and Tensing Norgay
- Who wrote 'The Lord of the Rings'?
  J.R.R. Tolkien
- Which Austrian actor was also Governor of California?
  Arnold Schwarzenegger
- Who painted 'Sunflowers'?
  Vincent van Gogh
- Who sang 'We all Live in a Yellow Submarine'?
  The Beatles

3.3   Spot the difference!

1.   In picture B the door of the garden shed is open.
2.   In picture A there is a bird flying towards the nest carrying a worm in its beak, but not in picture B.
3.   In picture B the garden gnome standing at the foot of the tree is holding a lantern in his left hand. (In picture A he is holding a bucket).
4.   In picture B there is a lawn mower on the lawn.
     In picture A there is a wheelbarrow.
5.   There are weeds growing through the ground in picture A.
6.   In picture B the cockerel on top of the shed is asleep.
7.   In picture A there is a T-shirt on the washing line.
8.   In picture A you can see water in the well. In picture B you can't see any water.
9.   In picture B there are 9 molehills on the lawn.
10. In picture B there is no ladder leaning against the tree.

3.5   A tall story

Mistakes:

1. Christmas cards are not sent in August.
2. Santa Claus doesn't deliver Christmas cards.
3. Rudolf is not a unicorn, but a reindeer.
4. Christmas cards are not thrown down the chimney.
5. Christmas songs called 'Christmas carols'.
6. 'We wish you a Merry Christmas'.
7. Mistletoe
8. You are supposed to kiss them.
9. The big Christmas celebration is on the 25th of December.
10. It is called 'Christmas dinner'.
11. Roast turkey
12. Christmas pudding

4.4   Odd one out

Common sound		Odd word out
1.	/iː/	suit
2.	/aɪ/	virtual
3.	/ʌ/	tune
4.	/ɜː/	fear
5.	/ɔː/	road
6.	/ə/	comb
7.	/əʊ/	through
8.	/eə/	fear
9.	/ɪə/	bear
10.	/aʊ/	lower
11.	/uː/	sew
12.	/ɑː/	mast
13.	/eɪ/	height

4.6   Phonemic word searches

Word search animals

Animals

dog, tiger, hedgehog, cat, tortoise, rat, hamster, snake, bear, boar, bat, cow, sow, mouse
(The first letter of each word is shaded darker)

k	d	əʊ	k	e	t	tʃ	r	e	h
eɪ	ɔɪ	m	aʊ	s	ʊ	ʌ	æ	dʒ	e
n	r	ə	s	ə	t	ɔ:	t	ə	dʒ
s	ɔ:	s	t	aʊ	dʒ	æ	ʌ	p	h
h	t	eə	æ	m	ɪ	r	ʃ	k	ɒ
ʌ	æ	b	ʊ	d	b	ɔ:	l	e	g
s	k	n	ʃ	h	æ	m	s	t	ə
b	ɪ	g	ə	ə	t	aʊ	p	ʊ	ʃ
b	æ	dʒ	æ	t	aɪ	g	ə	r	e
k	ɔ:	r	dʒ	æ	ʃ	u	g	ɒ	d

Other (non-animal) words

k	d	əʊ	k	e	t	tʃ	r	e	h
eɪ	ɔɪ	m	aʊ	s	ʊ	ʌ	æ	dʒ	e
n	r	ə	s	ə	t	ɔ:	t	ə	dʒ
s	ɔ:	s	t	aʊ	dʒ	æ	ʌ	p	h
h	t	eə	æ	m	ɪ	r	ʃ	k	ɒ
ʌ	æ	b	ʊ	d	b	ɔ:	l	e	g
s	k	n	ʃ	h	æ	m	s	t	ə
b	ɪ	g	ə	ə	t	aʊ	p	ʊ	ʃ
b	æ	dʒ	æ	t	aɪ	g	ə	r	e
k	ɔ:	r	dʒ	æ	ʃ	u	g	ɒ	d

(The first letter of each word is shaded darker)

code	god	sauce	taught	cane
shed	ham	tear	more	leg
big	push	badge	at	tie
core	or	hedge	law	guy

4.7 Phonemic word maze

START						
mails	eats	chants	parents	dies	animals	runs
dogs	friends	boys	nights	goats	tricks	hats
cats	rocks	holidays	tents	bikes	cooks	streets
books	it's	girls	helps	necks	potions	fits
answers	worms	learns	bagpipes	days	brooms	learned
apples	bakes	nuts	risks	times	bikes	sounds
hands	days	sits	talks	trees	hats	has
hits	babies	goes	takes	roses	toilets	heads
creatures	sits	colours	prizes	arms	bats	cabs
						FINISH

111

6.1   Looks familiar

You should have a three-digit number. The first digit is your original number, the second and third digits are your age!

6.3   All the same ...

The answer is 10

Appendices

A1.   Quiz clues (easy)

What word beginning with A ...

are elephants, hamsters and monkeys?	animals
is a fruit?	apple
is the opposite of before?	after
is the opposite of never?	always
comes between July and September?	August
is the month between March and May?	April
do you do with a question?	ask
is your dad's sister?	aunt

What word beginning with B ...

is the opposite of good?	bad
is the room where you brush your teeth?	bathroom
is the opposite of after?	before
is the opposite of in front of?	behind
has got wings?	bird
is the superlative form of good?	best
do you ride?	bike
is only one day in the year?	birthday

What word beginning with C ...

is the opposite of warm?	cold
is a long, thin orange vegetable?	carrot
do English people eat with fish?	chips
do children like to eat very much?	chocolate
do children like because of the presents?	Christmas
are blue, yellow and red?	colours
do you do when you're sad?	cry
do you do with knives and scissors?	cut

What word beginning with D ...

is the opposite of easy?	difficult
comes between November and January?	December
do you sometimes do when you sleep?	dream
do sometimes women wear?	dress
do you do with milk?	drink
do you call the one that you love?	darling

What word beginning with E ...

do you hear with?	ears
is two plus two plus six minus two?	eight
has got a long grey trunk?	elephant
is the opposite of beginning?	end
do you see with?	eyes
is the opposite of nobody?	everybody

What word beginning with F ...

are bananas, apples and oranges?	fruits
lives in the water and on land?	frog
lives in the water?	fish
is a game where you kick a ball towards a goal?	football
do you wear your shoes on?	feet
is married to your mother?	father
is the opposite of slow?	fast
is two times two?	four

What word beginning with G ...

are we playing now?	game
is in front of a house?	garden
is a window made of?	glass
goes with better and best?	good

| is your mum's sister's dad/mum? | grandmother |
| is an instrument with strings? | guitar |

What word beginning with H ...

can be blond?	hair
is 50% of something?	half
does the Easter rabbit do with the eggs?	hide
can you ride?	horse
is a thousand divided by ten?	hundred
does your finger do when you cut it?	hurt
are you when you want to eat something?	hungry

What word beginning with I ...

is frozen water?	ice
is the opposite of boring?	interesting
are you when you are not healthy?	ill

What word beginning with J ...

is something you wear?	jacket, jeans
do you put on your bread?	jam
is the month before August?	July
is the sixth month of the year?	June
do tigers live in?	jungle

What word beginning with K ...

is the queen's husband?	king
goes with spoon and fork?	knife
is a part of your leg?	knee
do you use for locking doors?	key
is a room where you cook?	kitchen

What word beginning with L ...

is the opposite of heavy?	light
is the opposite of early?	late
do you do if somebody tells you a joke?	laugh
is the capital of England?	London
is the opposite of hate?	love
do you do with your eyes?	look

What word beginning with M ...

is between February and April?	March
is the first day of the week?	Monday
is a month with three letters?	May
goes in between small and large?	medium
is the opposite of plus?	minus
is your dad's wife?	mother
is a small animal?	mouse

What word beginning with N ...

is the opposite of far?	near
is the opposite of old?	new
is in the middle of your face?	nose
is between October and December?	November
is when it's dark outside?	night
is three times three?	nine

What word beginning with O ...

is the opposite of young?	old
do you do with a closed door?	open
is a fruit and a colour?	orange
is the opposite of under?	over

What word beginning with P ...

do you write on?	paper
are your mum and dad?	parents
do you write with?	pen, pencil
are a hamster, a rabbit and a goldfish?	pets
is an instrument?	piano
is an animal?	pig
is a bird?	parrot
is a colour?	purple
is the opposite of minus?	plus

What word beginning with Q ...

is the opposite of slow?	quick
is the opposite of loud?	quiet
is the noise a duck makes?	quack
is something that you ask?	question

What word beginning with R ...

is an animal with long ears?	rabbit
has got many different colours?	rainbow
do you do with a book?	read
do you do with horses and bikes?	ride
is a colour?	red
is the opposite of wrong and left?	right
does a telephone do?	ring
is a circle?	round

What word beginning with S ...

do you do when you're not awake?	sleep, snore
is the opposite of quick?	slow
do you do when you're happy?	sing
is another word for talk?	speak

is the opposite of weak?	strong
goes with spring, autumn and winter?	summer
is the day between Saturday and Monday?	Sunday
is chocolate?	sweet
is your parents' child, but not your brother?	sister
is a kind of winter sport?	skiing

What word beginning with *T* ...

is the opposite of give?	take
is someone who is not small?	tall
is played with a yellow ball?	tennis
comes after Wednesday?	Thursday
are at the end of your feet?	toes
does a watch tell you?	time
is a red vegetable?	tomato
is the opposite of bottom?	top
do you have to brush every morning?	teeth

What word beginning with *U* ...

is the opposite of happy?	unhappy
is the opposite of over?	under
is what you don't do when somebody talks too fast?	understand

What word beginning with *V* ...

are onions, tomatoes and cucumbers?	vegetables
is the capital of Austria?	Vienna
is smaller than a town?	village
do you do if somebody is in hospital?	visit

What word beginning with *W* ...

might you have to do at a bus stop?	wait
is what you do with Christmas presents?	wrap
is what you do in the morning?	wake up

do you do in the bathroom every day?	wash
do you do with the TV?	watch
is you and me?	we

A2.   Quiz clues (difficult)

What word beginning with A ...

is a country in North Africa?	Algeria
is a synonym for 'very old'?	ancient
is the opposite of 'fake'?	authentic
is something which is precise?	accurate
travels into space?	astronaut
lived in Wonderland?	Alice

What word beginning with B ...

is a country, the capital of which is Sofia?	Bulgaria
is a colloquial word for 'mad'?	bats/bonkers
are clothes that are too big?	baggy
are eagles, budgies and hawks?	birds
had a partner called Robin?	Batman

What word beginning with C ...

is the former name of Sri Lanka?	Ceylon
will be the next king of England?	Charles
is a synonym for cold?	chilly
are Luxemburg, Iceland and India?	countries
are Brie, Cheddar and Roquefort?	cheeses

What word beginning with D ...

is a cathedral city in the north of England?	Durham
is a synonym for a catastrophe?	disaster
is something which tastes really good?	delicious

are rabies, malaria and cholera?	diseases
works by boring?	dentist
is the name of a famous cartoon duck?	Donald

What word beginning with E ...

is a continent?	Europe
is a synonym for serious?	earnest
is something which can be stretched?	elastic
fixes your cooker when it breaks down?	electrician

What word beginning with F ...

is something which is cat-like?	feline
are salmon, sharks and stingrays?	fish
is the opposite of clear?	fuzzy
comes when your house is burning?	firefighter

What word beginning with G ...

is a large city in Scotland?	Glasgow
is a synonym for horrible?	ghastly
are draughts, ludo and bridge?	games

What word beginning with H ...

is Budapest the capital of?	Hungary
was the English king who lost the Battle of Hastings?	Harold
is a synonym for good-looking?	handsome
is the opposite of clearly visible?	hidden
are thyme, basil and parsley?	herbs

What word beginning with I ...

is the name of the town where the	Ironbridge

120

world's first iron bridge was built?
is a synonym for stupid?   idiotic
is the opposite of unintelligent?   intelligent
is something which is not real?   imaginary
translates spoken language?   interpreter

What word beginning with *J* ...

did Guy Fawkes try to assassinate?   James I
is a synonym for nervous?   jumpy
is a very ripe peach?   juicy
are postman, secretary and teacher?   jobs
looks after the school building?   janitor
are berries used to make gin?   juniper

What word beginning with *K* ...

is a princess's father?   king
is a synonym for most important?   key
is the opposite of mean?   kind
describes a person who knows a lot?   knowledgeable
steals people?   kidnapper

What word beginning with *L* ...

is the museum where the Mona Lisa is kept? Louvre
is the capital of Peru?   Lima
is an adjective meaning 'recently died'?   late
is the most southerly Baltic state?   Lithuania

What word beginning with *M* ...

is the opposite of single?   married
is something which is tuneful?   melodious
are lasagne, fish and chips and curry?   meals
mends your car?   mechanic

can be water or honey?   melon

What word beginning with N ...

is one of the two poles?   North
is a synonym for pleasant?   nice
is a doctor for diseases of the brain?   neurologist
is something which hasn't been looked after? neglected
are hazel, brazil and chest...?   nuts
works in a hospital?   nurse

What word beginning with O ...

is a colour associated with Holland?   orange
is a synonym for extrovert?   outgoing
are hot and cold, wet and dry, tall and small? opposites
sells you glasses?   optician
is a fruit and a colour?   orange

What word beginning with P ...

comes after North and South to describe a
cold and icy area?   Pole
is a synonym for faultless?   perfect
is a synonym for much-liked?   popular
is the opposite of rude?   polite
brings your letters?   postman
grows in a pod?   peas

What word beginning with Q ...

is an Arab country?   Qatar
is a French-speaking province of Canada?   Quebec
is a synonym for old-fashioned?   quaint
is the opposite of noisy?   quiet

What word beginning with **R** ...

is the former name of Zimbabwe?	Rhodesia
is a verb meaning to turn in a circle?	rotate
goes after 'horse' to give us the name of a root vegetable?	radish
is the opposite of polite?	rude

What word beginning with **S** ...

is the capital of Sweden?	Stockholm
wrote 'As You Like It'?	Shakespeare
is a synonym for rarely?	seldom
is the opposite of deep?	shallow
is a person who thinks only of themselves?	selfish
operates on people?	surgeon

What word beginning with **T** ...

is the capital of Estonia?	Tallinn
is where Dracula comes from?	Transylvania
is a synonym for boring?	tedious
is the opposite of important?	trivial
describes a grateful person?	thankful
are hammers, drills and chisels?	tools

What word beginning with **U** ...

is a means of transport in London?	Underground
are Oxford and Cambridge famous for?	universities
is the opposite of happy?	unhappy
is the opposite of legal?	unlawful
is something which is incomplete?	unfinished

What word beginning with *V* ...

is a river in Russia?	Volga
is a synonym for empty?	vacant
is the opposite of tiny?	vast
is a person who has won something?	victor
are trains, cars and lorries?	vehicles
heals sick animals?	vet

What word beginning with *W* ...

is the opposite of east?	west
is a synonym for incorrect?	wrong
is the opposite of tame?	wild
is a road which is not straight?	winding
is a drink made from grapes?	wine

What word beginning with *Z* ...

used to be called Rhodesia?	Zimbabwe
is a place where wild animals are kept?	zoos
studies wild animals?	zoologist

A3. Game cards for colloquial English

Adjectives

Choose the correct answer - A, B, C or D.	Choose the correct answer - A, B, C or D.
Someone who is 'stuck-up' ... A. is short of cash. B. has a very high opinion of themselves. C. is not feeling good. D. has just been arrested by the police. **B**	Someone who is 'skint'... A. is very absent-minded. B. is dead. C. is very thin. D. has no money. **D**

Choose the correct answer – A, B, C or D	Choose the correct answer – A, B, C or D
Unpleasant remarks are sometimes described as '...' A. doggy. B. catty. C. snaky. D. birdy. **B**	Someone who is lost for words is '...' A. mouthless. B. mouthsmacked. C. gobsmacked. D. closemouthed. **C**

Choose the correct answer – A, B, C or D	Choose the correct answer – A, B, C or D
If you are 'chuffed', you ... A. have been arrested. B. have locked yourself out of the house. C. have eaten too much. D. are very happy. **D**	A dangerous situation can be described as '...' A. curly. B. hairy. C. fluffy. D. bearded. **B**

Choose the correct answer – A, B, C or D	Choose the correct answer – A, B, C or D
A person who is confused and keeps forgetting things is ...	Looking 'sheepish' means looking ...
A. scatterminded.	A. untidy.
B. scatterheaded.	B. stupid.
C. scattervisioned.	C. sleepy.
D. scatterbrained.	D. embarrassed.
D	**D**

Choose the correct answer – A, B, C or D	Choose the correct answer – A, B, C or D
A 'scruffy' person is...	A 'tight-fisted' person is ...
A. super-intelligent.	A. mean.
B. long-haired.	B. tough.
C. unhappy.	C. nervous.
D. untidily dressed	D. angry.
D	**A**

Choose the correct answer – A, B, C or D	Choose the correct answer – A, B, C or D
Something which is 'duff' ...	A 'stroppy' person is ...
A. is smelly.	A. overweight.
B. gets on your nerves.	B. ugly.
C. is old-fashioned.	C. unreliable.
D. doesn't work properly.	D. bad-tempered.
D	**D**

A4. Topic cards for 60-second guessing game

HOBBIES	RELATIONS	PARTS OF THE BODY
1. swimming	1. mother	1. arm
2. football	2. father	2. knee
3. dancing	3. uncle	3. leg
4. cycling	4. nephew	4. toes
5. climbing	5. brother	5. thumb
6. tennis	6. sister	6. eyes
7. skiing	7. grandmother	7. chin
8. horse riding	8. aunt	8. cheek

SCHOOL THINGS	PETS	ROOMS OF THE HOUSE
1. ruler	1. dog	1. living room
2. exercise book	2. cat	2. dining room
3. folder	3. mouse	3. bedroom
4. scissors	4. guinea pig	4. spare room
5. calculator	5. budgie	5. kitchen
6. rubber	6. hamster	6. toilet
7. pencil	7. goldfish	7. bathroom
8. pen	8. parrot	8. cellar

A5.   Quiz clues: Words with two meanings

ball   is a round object used in games and also an organised dance?

bank   is a place where you can keep your money and a synonym for a 'slope'?

bar   is a place where you can stand and drink alcohol, and a synonym for 'forbid'?

bats   is a colloquial term for 'mad' and are small mammals?

bat   is used to play table tennis with and flies at night?

bark   would you find on a tree trunk and is the noise a dog makes?

bear   means 'to tolerate' and can be brown, black or white?

bill   is part of a bird and something you pay?

bit   is a small piece and something which is found in a horse's mouth?

blue   is depressed and a colour?

bolt   describes how a horse runs away quickly and is something you use to lock a door?

book   is something you read and a verb describing the process of reserving flights or rooms for a holiday?

bore   is a person who is extremely uninteresting and what the dentist does?

box   is a verb meaning 'to hit' and a container?

bowl   is something you eat out of and a heavy, asymmetrical wooden ball rolled along the ground in a popular game?

break	a short pause and a verb meaning 'to separate' into pieces'?
can	is beer sometimes sold in and a verb sometimes used to express ability?
change	is what you might get when you have paid for something in a shop, and a verb meaning 'to alter'?
chest	is part of your body and a large container?
clear	is easy to understand and transparent?
club	is an organisation for people with a common interest, and something you play golf with?
count	is to say a sequence of numbers out loud and the title of a vampire who lives in Transylvania?
cold	is a low temperature and something you can catch in winter?
cool	is a low temperature and something you think is great?
dip	is a short swim and a downwards movement?
down	is a duck's feathers and the opposite of 'up'?
drop	is a small amount of liquid and a verb that means 'to let something fall'?
duck	is what you do when you go through a low door so as not to bang your head and a bird that goes 'quack'?
faint	is a word meaning 'hardly visible' and also 'to lose consciousness'?
fair	is just and the opposite of 'dark' when talking about hair?
fan	supports a football team and keeps you cool?

fast	is a synonym for 'quick' and a verb meaning 'to do without food'?
fence	is a person who sells stolen goods and is what can divide two gardens?
file	do you use on your nails and is a place where you keep documents?
flat	can be a place where you live and a synonym for 'level'?
fly	do birds do, and is an insect?
fork	is a place where a road divides and something you use to eat?
funny	is something which is strange and something which makes you laugh?
game	is a deer or a stag and something that can be played?
green	is a synonym for 'inexperienced' and the colour associated with envy?
handle	means 'to cope with' and is also part of a suitcase?
head	is what your ears are attached to and the leader of an organisation?
hide	is to place something out of view and another word for an animal's skin?
iron	is a metal and a verb meaning 'to make clothes smooth by applying heat and pressure to them'?
jam	is when traffic comes to a standstill and something made from fruit you can spread on bread?
jerk	is an idiot and is a verb meaning 'to twitch'?
kid	is a young child and a young goat?

kind	is a type of something and a someone who is nice to you?
leaves	means 'departs' and falls off trees in autumn?
light	is not heavy or dark?
left	can mean 'remaining' and is the meaning of the Latin word 'sinister'?
lie	is to not tell the truth and when your body is on a flat surface?
mark	is your score on a test and also a word meaning 'to correct a test'?
mean	is not very nice and an arithmetical average?
mine	is a place to get diamonds and belongs to me?
nail	do you find at the end of your fingers and is something used to join pieces of wood together?
net	divides a tennis court and means how much salary you get after deductions such as tax and social insurance?
note	is the description of the pitch of a sound and something used to pay for things with?
organ	is a musical instrument and your liver?
odd	can mean 'strange' and also describes numbers such as 1, 3, 5 etc.?
palm	is a type of tree and the flat inner part of your hand?
park	is a large recreational area and what you do with your car?
paste	means 'to stick' and is a type of spread made of meat or fish?

pen	is an enclosure for sheep and something you write with?
plain	is a flat area and someone who is not very pretty?
play	is what children do with friends in the park and what actors perform in a theatre?
point	can you win in a tennis match and is what you do with your finger if you want to show somebody where something is?
pool	means to share money or ideas, and is a place to swim?
pound	is a unit of money and a verb meaning 'to hit hard and repeatedly'?
punch	is a verb meaning 'to hit' and a popular alcoholic drink at Christmas markets?
pupil	is part of your eye and goes to school?
racket	is a loud noise and a criminal scheme?
right	is the hand most people use to write with and a word meaning 'correct'?
ring	is something you wear on your finger, and a place where a boxing match takes place?
rock	is a stone and a type of music?
rose	is the past tense of a verb meaning 'to get up' and a flower?
ruler	is another word for a monarch and something which is used to measure things with?
saw	is used to cut wood and is the past tense of a verb meaning 'to observe'?
scales	does a fish have and a singer sing?

shake	is an uncontrollable movement and a drink made from milk?
shed	is a small building you might find in a garden and to take your clothes off, for example?
sink	is something you would find in the kitchen and what the Titanic did?
steer	means 'to direct a vehicle' and is another word for a bull?
sole	is a fish and on the bottom of your shoe?
space	would you travel to in a rocket and is an area with nothing in it?
spring	means 'to jump' and is a coil of wire used in mattresses?
squash	is a type of juice and a verb meaning 'to flatten'?
stable	is where a horse lives and a word meaning steady?
stamp	is to hit the ground hard with one foot and something you put on a letter?
stick with	is a long thin piece of wood and what you do glue?
store	means 'to keep for a long period of time' and is a place where you buy something?
stern	is 'severe' and the back of a boat?
tie	is a verb meaning 'to connect' and something you wear round your neck?
train	is a means of transport and is another word for 'to practise'?
trunk	can you pack things in when you travel and is part of an elephant?

type	is a category of something and also a verb meaning 'to use a keyboard to write'?
watch	is to observe and a thing you use to tell the time?
wave	is what you do with your arm when you see people from a distance and a word that describes the movement of water?
well	is a synonym for 'healthy' and a hole in the ground that you get water out of?
yard	is three feet and is a place behind a house?
yellow	is a colour and a synonym for 'cowardly'?

References

Bowen, T. & Marks, J. (1992) *The Pronunciation Book.* Longman

Buttner, A. (2007) *Activities, Games and Assessment Strategies for the Foreign Language Classroom.* Eye On Education

Council of Europe (2020) *Common European Framework of Reference for Languages: Learning, teaching, assessment – Companion volume.* Council of Europe Publishing, Strasbourg. www.coe.int/lang-cefr.

Harmer, J. (2001) *The Practice of English Language Teaching.* Longman

Hewings, M. (2007) *English Pronunciation in Use.* CUP

Lenneberg, E.H. (1967) *Biological Foundations of Language.* 1967 Wiley

Meighan, J. (2011) *Drama Start.* Jem Books 2011

Swan, M. & Walter, C. (1990) *New Cambridge Course.* Vol. 1. CUP

Ur, P. (2016) *Penny Ur's 100 Teaching Tips:* Cambridge Handbooks for Language Teachers CUP

Ur, P. (2014) *Discussions and More: Oral Fluency Practice in the Classroom.* Cambridge Handbooks for Language Teachers CUP

Wright, A., Betteridge, D., Buckby, M. (2016) *Games for Language Learning.* Cambridge Handbooks for Language Teachers CUP

Acknowledgements

It would be an unusual teacher who could claim to only ever use things in his lessons that he had invented himself. Teachers gather materials and ideas over the years and there are many activities in circulation whose precise origin has been lost in the mists of time or is not possible to ascertain. Where possible I have attributed sources which have inspired the activities in this book.

My thanks go to Harald Spann, for constructive advice and criticism, and proof-reading, thus demonstrating once again that his range of expertise extends well beyond the world of football, and also to Christina Stainthorpe and Julia Strauß for their help in proof-reading the text. Similarly, thanks go to Thomas Schöftner for help with all things technical and advice on e-learning matters. Any errors still to be found here are my own.

About the Author

 Neil Stainthorpe is a native English speaker, English teacher and teacher trainer with over 33 years experience at the Pädagogische Hochschule der Diözese Linz (formerly Pädagogische Akademie). He grew up in England in the West Midlands, then studied Modern Foreign Languages at the University of Leeds, before training to be an English teacher.

Additionally, he taught for many years at primary level, where he was able to combine guitar playing, singing and playing games, and managed to get away with calling it work. ☺

contact: neil.stainthorpe@ph-linz.at

Modern Canterbury Tales

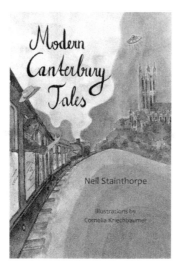

Late 14th century:
Geoffrey Chaucer's work 'The Canterbury Tales', tells the story of a group of pilgrims on their way to Canterbury. To pass the time, each agrees to tell a story connected with their life...

Early 21st century:
Once more, a group of travellers sets out on a pilgrimage to Canterbury. As on the original journey, all the members of this group, consisting of an anaesthetist, a postman, a flight attendant, and many more, have tales to tell, but somehow they don't seem to have got the right idea about what a pilgrimage is all about ...

As Easy as Falling off a Log!
Level – Upper intermediate/advanced
Available also as Kindle e-book

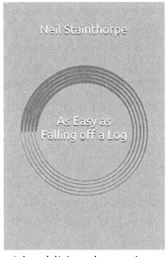

A quiz - journey through a collection of British English colloquial, everyday, idiomatic expressions.

What do 'skint', 'wonky' and 'gobsmacked' mean?

How does it feel to be 'as sick as a parrot'?

Is it a good thing if you get on with someone 'like a house on fire'?

300 everyday, colloquial English expressions in a fun quiz format with additional exercises.

The focus in this book is on learning new words and phrases in a fun way and then applying them in meaningful contexts. The book is divided into 30 chapters covering 10 words/phrases. The reader tries to guess the correct answer from a choice of four options. Having checked the correct answers to the quiz questions, the reader then applies the newly acquired vocabulary to a gapped-text exercise immediately following.

After chapters 5, 10, 15, 20, 25 and 30 there is a review section.

The aim is to introduce anybody who wants to understand spoken British English better to common expressions in everyday use in Great Britain in an entertaining and intrinsically motivating way.

Pigs Might Fly!

Advanced-level crosswords

Pigs might fly? Why?

Is flogging a dead horse a hare-brained scheme?

When you're stony broke, what might help more? A whip-round or a flutter?

A Brummie talking nineteen to the dozen? And blowing his own trumpet to boot? Would that drive you up the wall?

Broaden your range of vocabulary! Over 450 idioms, similes, colloquialisms and other common expressions.

Easy to learn! Simply fill in the crosswords! And check up on the correct usage in the glossary after each puzzle!

Modern Fairy Tales
Illustrations by Cornelia Kriechbaumer
Level – Upper intermediate/advanced
Available also as Kindle e-book

Modern Fairy Tales ... You thought you knew these stories? Not so! Find out ...

... how Cinderella gets the prince. (Unfortunately, he's not the sharpest knife in the drawer.)

... what happens when The Three Little Pigs get kicked out from home and go off to build their houses. Spending your evenings in the pub can be a life-saver!

... about Goldilocks and the three other bears. Cousins of the well-known porridge eating bears, these three greedy food inspectors travel round the countryside causing havoc. How to stop them?

Plus other tales you've never heard before!

A Massive Wooden Hammer
Level – Upper intermediate/advanced
Available also as Kindle e-book

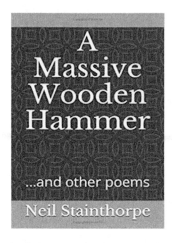

Have you ever …

… thought about using a hedgehog to solve your problems?

… been the victim of a conspiracy?

… wondered what fish think when they arrive at the fish market?

Then read on … and find out about learner drivers, complaining neighbours, students, camping holidays and of course the significance of the massive wooden hammer!

Murder on the Farm
Level – Upper intermediate/advanced
Available also as Kindle e-book

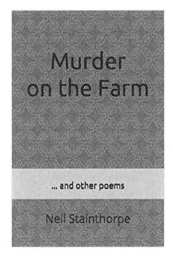

All is not well on the farm! What are the animals plotting? Does the farmer know about it? Have you ever been on a holiday that wasn't quite what you expected?

Do you really have a ball when you go to a ball?

Then read on ...! (... and also find out about New Year's resolutions, modern art, incompetent pilots and much more!)

The Great British Quiz Book
- An Introduction to Britain in 40 Activities
Neil Stainthorpe & Harald Spann

Level – Upper intermediate/advanced
Available also as Kindle e-book

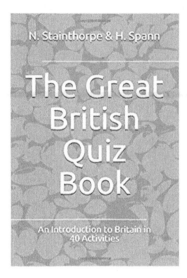

Britain is a fantastic place with fantastic people (yes, we know, there may be the odd exception).

In this book we would like to share our common fascination for this wonderful place, its people, traditions and customs. It is a mixture of a critical look at the 'nature of Britishness' (whatever that is) in part 1, followed by a wide range of interesting and fun activities, quizzes and facts in part 2. This book is for students and teachers of English, anybody who loves doing quizzes, crosswords and other puzzles and who wants to find out more about Britain in a fun way.

All books available on:
www.amazon.de / www.amazon.co.uk

Printed in Great Britain
by Amazon